THE ENCYCLOPEDIA OF
WOOD
WORKING
TECHNIQUES

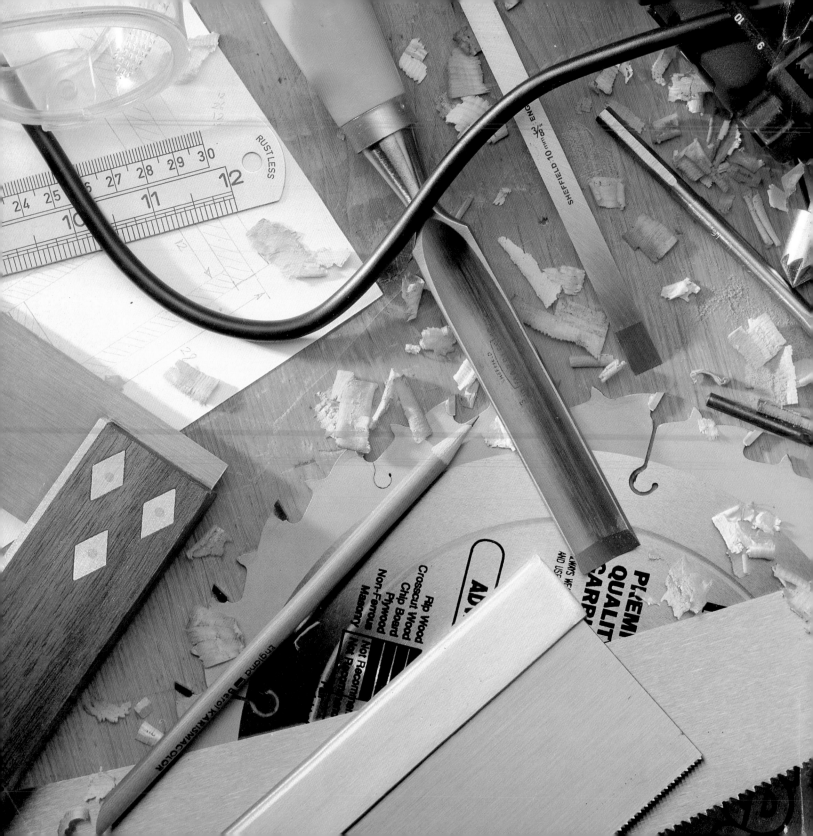

THE ENCYCLOPEDIA OF
WOOD WORKING TECHNIQUES

JEREMY BROUN

NEW
BURLINGTON
BOOKS

This book was designed and produced by
Quarto Inc
The Old Brewery
6 Blundell Street
London N7 9BH

Senior editor Kate Kirby
Editors Mike Collins, Lydia Derbyshire, Bob Flexner
Senior art editors Phillip Gilderdale, Mark Stevens
Designer Bill Mason
Photographers Jermey Brown, Paul Forrester, Chas Wilder
Illustrations Graham Rosewarn
Picture manager Rebecca Horsewood
Art editor Moira Clinch
Publishing director Janet Slingsby

Publishers Note:
Woodworking can be dangerous. Both hand and power tools can quickly sever
nerves, tendons, or limbs. Allways read the
instruction manuals and use the safety guards provided; for the purposes of
photography, many of the guards were removed, but this is not a recomended
procedure.

As far as the methods and techniques mentioned in this book are concerned,
all statements, information, and advice given here are believed to be true and
accurate. However, neither the author, copyright holder, nor the publisher can
accept any legal liability for errors or ommisions

The furniture and decorative woodwork shown in this book are the copyright
of the individual artists, and may not be reproduced for commercial purposes.

Special thanks to Ian Styles of Axminster Power Tool Centre, Ian Howes for
help with photography, Andrew Varah, Nick Gibbs.

Typeset by West End Studios, Eastbourne
Manufactured in Hong Kong by Regent Publishing Services Ltd.
Printed in China by Lee-Fung Asco Printers Ltd.

CONTENTS

INTRODUCTION

Wood never ceases to fascinate and engage us. It is man's oldest natural resource, and the diverse ways in which it has been fashioned over the centuries tell the story of civilization better than any other material. From tribal masks to wheels, pit props to paper for books, wood is unique.

As a material, it has remarkable character – it bends, it twists, it splits, it swells, it shrinks, it is fragrant, it can be almost transparent. It can be hard, soft, rigid or springy. It can last for centuries, or it can perish in seconds in fire.

There is hardly anything that has not been made of wood, and there is hardly anyone who is not drawn to its tactile and visual qualities. The infinite variety in the grain of wood has universal appeal, and it has enormous versatility both as a structural and decorative medium. It is one of the most popular materials to be fashioned today by both amateurs and professionals alike.

The traditions and techniques associated with woodworking have survived for centuries, and I believe that a mastery of technique underpins successful woodworking. I was fortunate enough to receive a firm grounding in hand-working techniques, and this fired my passion for designing in wood. The power-tool revolution has not negated the old methods, but simply modified our approach. All tools, both hand and power operated, are a joy to work with, provided they are skillfully handled. I hope this book goes some way toward explaining how this can be achieved.

Wood is a wonderful and satisfying material to use. Whenever you use it, you will learn something new. Do not be put off by your lack of knowledge or experience, and do not be deterred by a fear of failure. Failure is an essential step to subsequent success. No number of words or photographs can tell you or show you what it is that makes the perfect joint – that you will find out for yourself as you work with different woods in different pieces, and, when you have acquired the "knack," your confidence will grow and your command of technique will increase, enabling you to experiment still further with new designs.

HOW TO USE THIS BOOK

The book offers an integrated approach to wood. The first part deals with important basic techniques and offers a detailed analysis of the "nuts and bolts" of woodworking. The second part, Themes, is devoted to the techniques in action, with examples of some of the best work to have been produced around the world; these pieces should inspire you to try out the techniques for yourself.

Ordering of material
Techniques are listed in alphabetical order to enable you to find your way around.

Crossreferences
Where appropriate text and captions use small capital letter crossreferences to denote other useful and applicable techniques; crossreferences occur in the Themes section too, to enable you to relate the working method to the end result.

Checklists
The checklists show at a glance the key items of equipment needed to carry out a particular technique.

Essentials: basic tools you will need whether you are using hand or power methods.

Hand tools

Power tools

Health and safety notes

Text
Each technique has a short introductory section discussing key features of the techniques and special points to bear in mind.

Demonstrations
Techniques are explained using step-by-step demonstrations. These demonstrations are divided into small units, showing different aspects of the technique.

Hand and power tools
Where appropriate, both techniques are demonstrated.

HEALTH AND SAFETY

No subject has come to public attention in recent years more than health and safety. The popularity of woodworking and the subsequent increase in the numbers of people involved in the activity have inevitably led to more accidents. Although legislation has been introduced to cover industrial and educational establishments, home woodworkers, who are usually working alone, are left to exercise their own discretion.

Health and safety should primarily be a matter of common sense, and no amount of legislation or safety guards on machines can prevent someone from cutting off a finger with a saw or severing a nerve by allowing a chisel to slip. Manufacturers invariably provide clear and comprehensive instructions for the safe operation of the tools and equipment they produce, and these should always be read carefully before any item is used.

However, health and safety also includes taking precautions against the dangers that can arise through dust and debris, and through noise pollution. Eye and ear protectors are essential and should always be worn. In addition, not only should you wear a respirator, but you should also use equipment that extracts dust at the source. Noise pollution can be minimized by insulating individual pieces of equipment and, of course, the workshop itself.

Perhaps the greatest risk in the home workshop is from fire. Always sweep up dust and chips at the end of the day and dispose of them carefully.

CHECKLIST

Power tools

● Always follow the manufacturer's instructions.

● When working with machinery, never wear loose clothing and tie back long hair.

● Keep hands well away from moving or cutting edges.

● Wear ear protectors and goggles, especially when working a spindle molder or power planer.

● Beware of trailing cables when using hand-held machinery.

● Always unplug the equipment before adjusting machinery.

● If in doubt read or get some tuition before using any unfamiliar tools.

● Be sure all power tools and machines are correctly wired and insulated before use.

Workshop environment

● Keep the workshop well ventilated at all times.

● Always use a dust mask or face shield in a dusty atmosphere.

● Be neat; this saves time and prevents accidents.

● Always store flammable chemicals, lacquers, varnish, etc., in a cool, safe place.

Using chemicals

● Avoid all skin contact with chemicals and glues.

● Wear gloves and goggles when using or mixing chemicals.

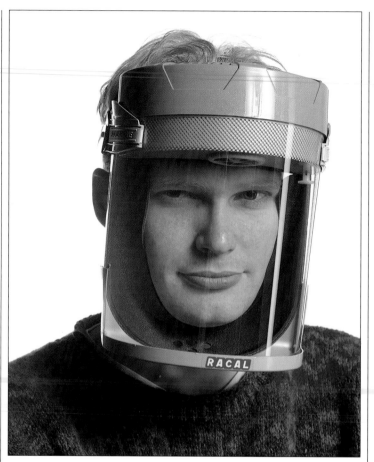

All-in-one respirator/face shield

The lightweight and convenient all-in-one respirator/face shield is a fairly recent development. The unit blows a gentle stream of air through a replaceable filter into the face-mask cavity and thereby prevents dust from entering. It is powered by a battery that can be carried on the belt or attached to the unit itself. The battery pack will last for a full working day, and the visor has a detachable, clear plastic protective overlay.

Dust mask
▶ It is always worth buying the best possible quality dust mask. Some brands are less effective than others, especially if they do not fit snugly around the contour of your nose. Make sure that you choose masks that have a nose clip as an integral part of their design.

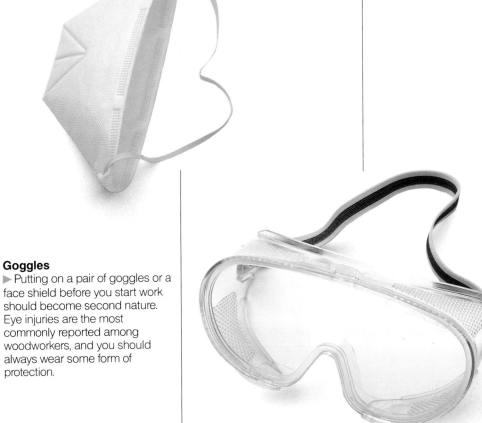

Goggles
▶ Putting on a pair of goggles or a face shield before you start work should become second nature. Eye injuries are the most commonly reported among woodworkers, and you should always wear some form of protection.

Hearing protectors
You should wear earplugs or hearing protectors to protect your hearing from long-term damage whenever you use power tools such as saws and routers. These soft, padded protectors are inexpensive, and it should soon become a matter of habit to put them on.

HAND TOOLS

Most woodworking tools are hand-held – indeed, woodworking is itself a manual activity. However, tools that are operated by the muscles rather than an external power source are defined as "hand tools." When time is pressing, you may prefer to use a powered tool, but there are occasions when it is both quicker and more efficient to use a hand tool – when machines have to be set up, for instance – and hand tools are vital in MEASURING AND LAYING OUT, for no power tool – apart from a robot – can perform these tasks.

Some woodworkers prefer to use hand tools and to "feel" the wood they are using with their fingers.

Hand tools are, in any case, an essential part of the kit of all woodworkers, and one of the great pleasures in woodworking is building up a collection of personal tools.

▼ The try square is a vital piece of equipment. It is used for marking and checking lines at 90 degrees, and various sizes are available.

Try square

Sliding bevel

Miter square

▼ A coping saw is essential for cutting fine, straight, or curved lines, especially for removing waste from dovetails, where a tenon saw is too large.

▶ A Sliding bevel can be set at any angle for marking and checking angles on wood.

▶ The miter square, with its blade set at 45 degrees, is used for marking and checking.

Coping saw

▶ A tenon saw is the best general-purpose saw for cutting straight lines. They are usually 12 inches long and have 13-15 teeth per inch. A dovetail saw (far right) is a miniature tenon saw for finer work. They are about 8 inches long and have 16-22 teeth per inch.

Tenon saw

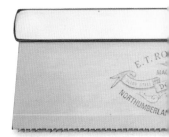

▶A beech marking gauge is used to mark parallel lines. The stock is held firm against the edge of the wood, while the spur is trailed across the surface.

▶A mortise gauge or combined mortise and marking gauge as it is sometimes known, has a single spur and two movable spurs, which can be set to the width of a mortise chisel. The stock is then held in position with its locking screw.

▼Handsaws are either rip, crosscut, or general purpose for cutting straight lines along or across the grain. They are approximately 25 inches long and have 6-8 teeth per inch.

Handsaw

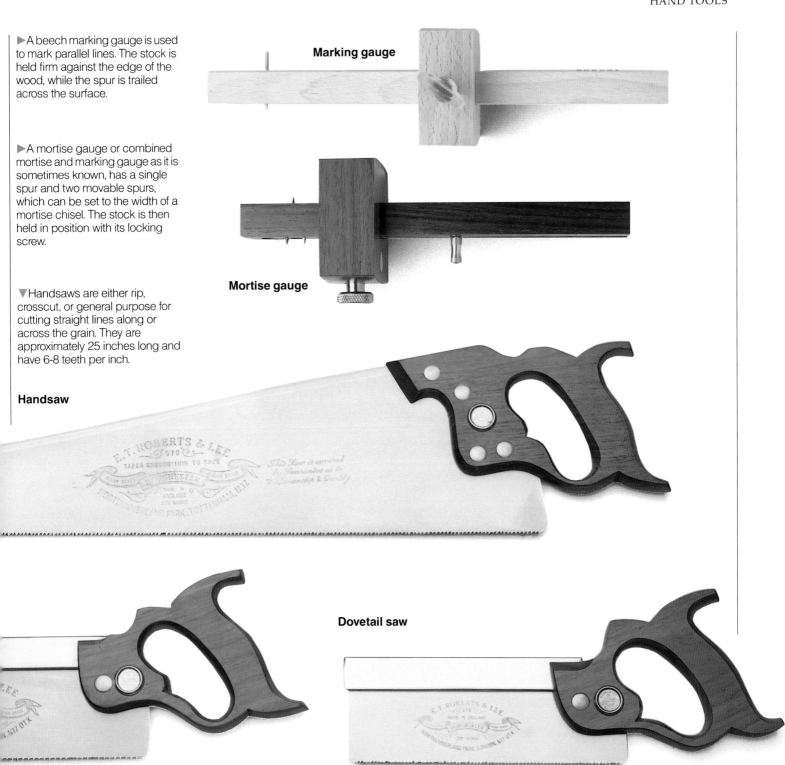

Marking gauge

Mortise gauge

Dovetail saw

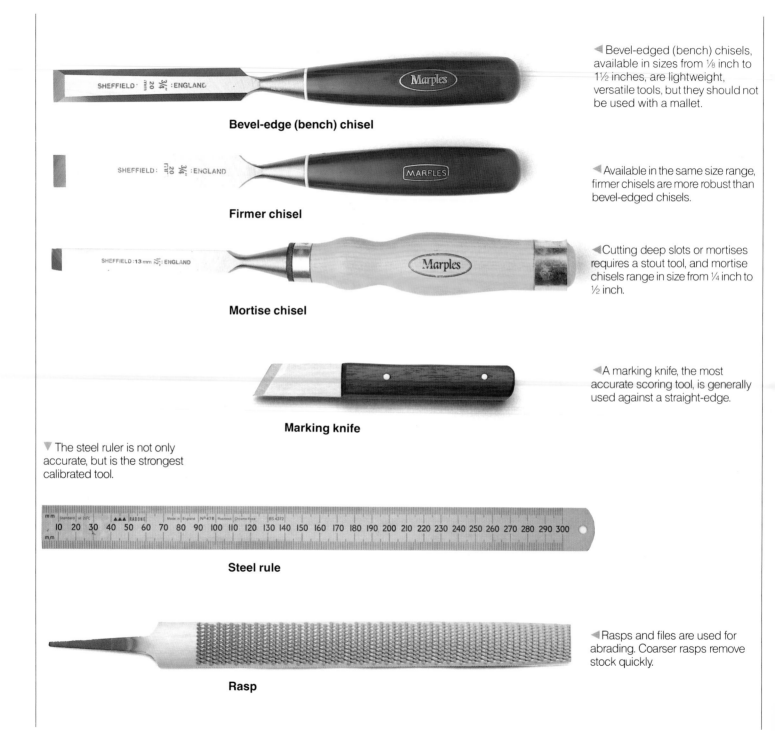

Bevel-edge (bench) chisel

◀ Bevel-edged (bench) chisels, available in sizes from ⅛ inch to 1½ inches, are lightweight, versatile tools, but they should not be used with a mallet.

Firmer chisel

◀ Available in the same size range, firmer chisels are more robust than bevel-edged chisels.

Mortise chisel

◀ Cutting deep slots or mortises requires a stout tool, and mortise chisels range in size from ¼ inch to ½ inch.

Marking knife

◀ A marking knife, the most accurate scoring tool, is generally used against a straight-edge.

▼ The steel ruler is not only accurate, but is the strongest calibrated tool.

Steel rule

Rasp

◀ Rasps and files are used for abrading. Coarser rasps remove stock quickly.

Spokeshave

▲For accurate shaping there is little to beat the spokeshave, which can have a flat or a rounded sole.

Smoothing plane

▶About 9 inches long, the steel smoothing plane, with its fine blade adjustments, is a vital tool for flat and shaped skimming.

▼The smaller blockplane, which has a shallower blade angle, is used for delicate work.

Blockplane

▲The jack plane, which can be 13¾-15¼ inches long, makes long pieces truer, and the extra weight gives more control.

Jack plane

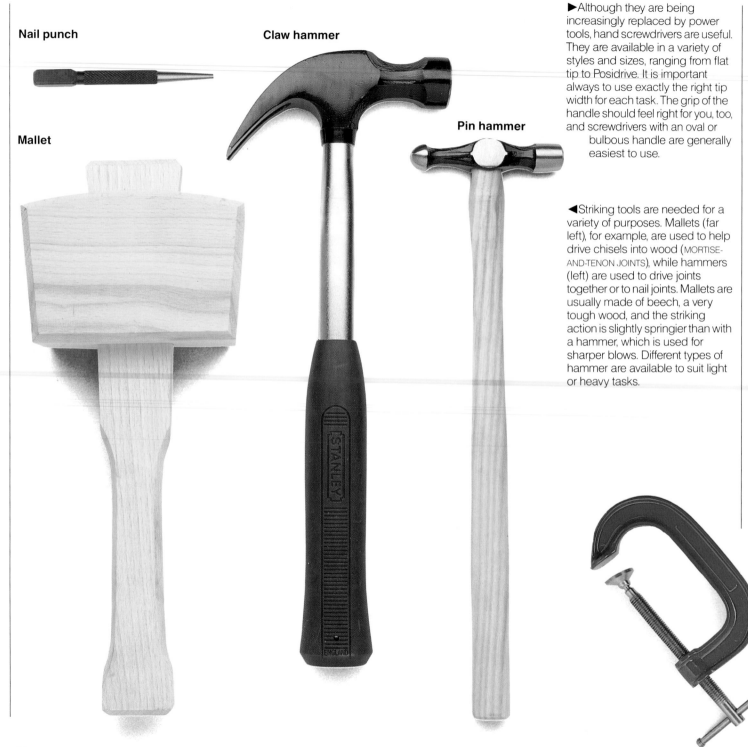

Nail punch

Claw hammer

Mallet

Pin hammer

►Although they are being increasingly replaced by power tools, hand screwdrivers are useful. They are available in a variety of styles and sizes, ranging from flat tip to Posidrive. It is important always to use exactly the right tip width for each task. The grip of the handle should feel right for you, too, and screwdrivers with an oval or bulbous handle are generally easiest to use.

◄Striking tools are needed for a variety of purposes. Mallets (far left), for example, are used to help drive chisels into wood (MORTISE-AND-TENON JOINTS), while hammers (left) are used to drive joints together or to nail joints. Mallets are usually made of beech, a very tough wood, and the striking action is slightly springier than with a hammer, which is used for sharper blows. Different types of hammer are available to suit light or heavy tasks.

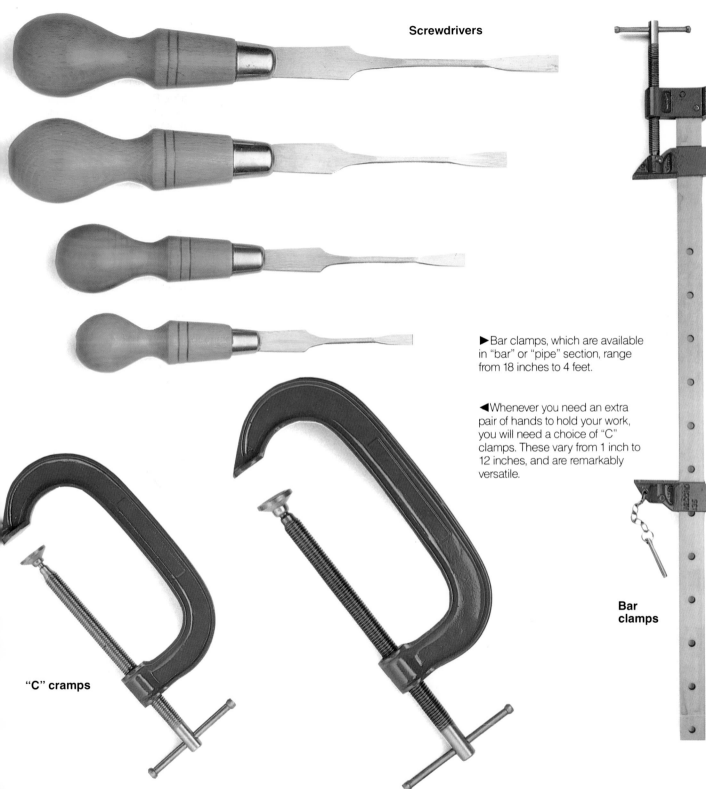

Screwdrivers

▶Bar clamps, which are available in "bar" or "pipe" section, range from 18 inches to 4 feet.

◀Whenever you need an extra pair of hands to hold your work, you will need a choice of "C" clamps. These vary from 1 inch to 12 inches, and are remarkably versatile.

Bar clamps

"C" cramps

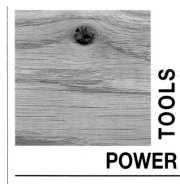

POWER TOOLS

In the past few decades, the development of power tools has changed the face of woodworking. Not only do these tools remove the drudgery from such arduous tasks as drilling and planing, but the technology offers new ways in which wood can be fashioned – by the router, for instance. The development of aluminum casting, plastic molding and silicon chip technology has brought the power tool a long way from the simple portable drill or drill attachment. Improvements in the electric motor and advances in cutting technology – tungsten-carbide tipped (TCT) blades, for example – have also been significant. Most recently, cordless tools have provided the woodworker with a new range of convenient and compact tools.

►A vertical drill stand will accommodate a portable drill with a 1¾-inch collar and permit more accurate drilling.

▼ The portable electric drill is the original power tool, and there can be few home workshops without one. With a keyed or fast-action chuck, a cord-powered drill should operate on 550 watts with a ½-inch chuck.

Drill stand with drill

►Twist drill-bits, which range from ¹⁄₆₄ to ½ inch and which can have center points, are used for general work.

Drill-bits

▼Flat-bits (spade bits) make it possible to cut larger holes but using a narrow ¼-inch shank. They are available from ¼-1½ inches.

Portable electric drill

BOSCH CSB 550-2
550 W · Beton Ø max. 15 mm

Flat-bits

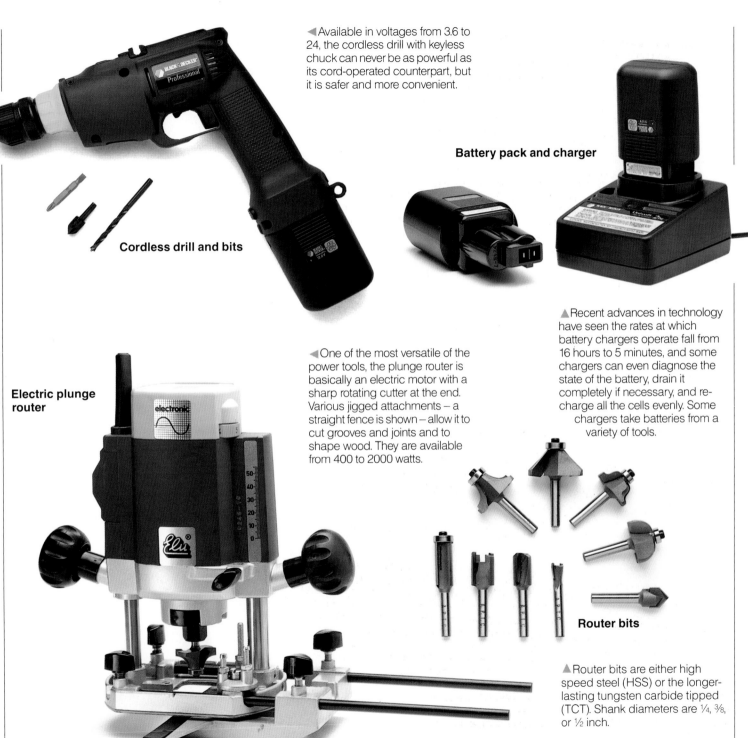

◄Available in voltages from 3.6 to 24, the cordless drill with keyless chuck can never be as powerful as its cord-operated counterpart, but it is safer and more convenient.

Battery pack and charger

Cordless drill and bits

▲Recent advances in technology have seen the rates at which battery chargers operate fall from 16 hours to 5 minutes, and some chargers can even diagnose the state of the battery, drain it completely if necessary, and re-charge all the cells evenly. Some chargers take batteries from a variety of tools.

Electric plunge router

◄One of the most versatile of the power tools, the plunge router is basically an electric motor with a sharp rotating cutter at the end. Various jigged attachments – a straight fence is shown – allow it to cut grooves and joints and to shape wood. They are available from 400 to 2000 watts.

Router bits

▲Router bits are either high speed steel (HSS) or the longer-lasting tungsten carbide tipped (TCT). Shank diameters are ¼, ⅜, or ½ inch.

Jigsaw

Jigsaw blades

Oilstone

▲ The jigsaw is a versatile hand-held tool for making straight, curved, or angled cuts. The blade moves up and down, and the cut is more efficient when the action is "orbital." Different blades are available for use with different materials.

▲ The combination oilstone (top) has coarse/medium or medium/fine grit surfaces. It is lubricated with oil and used to sharpen chisels and plane blades. The diamond stone has a grid of durable diamond particles set in plastic.

▼ The portable circular saw is used to cut solid wood or manufactured board material. A straight fence can be attached for parallel cuts. The blade can be set to different depths for grooving, and the sole plate tilted for angled cuts along and across the grain. Blades are 5-9 inches in diameter

Portable circular saw

Random orbit sander

Orbital sander

▲The random orbit sander has a self-gripping backed abrasive disk, which moves eccentrically while it rotates to create a random abrading effect. It is used for flat and curved work.

▲The orbital sander uses ½ or ⅓ size abrasive sheets, which are clamped to a padded baseplate. The action is elliptical, and the tool should be used under its own weight.

▼A belt sander uses a 3 or 4 inch continuous belt for heavy-duty abrading.

Biscuit jointer

Belt sander

▲The biscuit jointer offers a versatile method of connecting solid board or sheet wood. The blade of a small circular saw is plunged to form elliptical recesses into which compressed wood "biscuits" are glued.

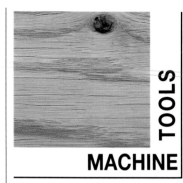

MACHINE TOOLS

Not many years ago, a powered planer or table saw would have weighed tons and would have taken up so much space in a workshop that there would have been no room for anything else. Today, the availability of small powered machine tools has made precise and imaginative work possible for both amateurs and professionals. Cast aluminum has replaced heavy steel in the manufacture of the components, and the efficiency of the motors has increased as their size has diminished. Some, such as the mini-planer-thicknessers, have become so small that they are as portable as hand power tools. Others, such as the spindle molder, can perform the same tasks and have the same capacity as some of the largest electric routers.

The variety and portability of the modern, lightweight machine tools makes planning and setting up a workshop much easier. When you are placing these tools, you must leave space for the "infeed" and "outfeed" of the wood, but, if space is limited, remember that not all these tools have to be bolted to the floor, and they can be moved into position when they are needed.

All woodworking tools, especially powered items, are potentially dangerous. Strict safety procedures should always be followed, including the positioning of safety guards, whenever they are used.

Bandsaw

Bench grinder

◄The bench grinder has coarse- and medium-grit wheels for repairing the edges of chisels and plane blades and touching up drill-bits. Non-ferrous metals should not be used on grinders, because they will clog the wheels. Keep a jar of water nearby for cooling, because considerable heat is generated by grinding steel.

▲The bandsaw is an extremely useful machine. It can cut both straight and curved lines with the table fixed at 90 degrees or tilted to up to 45 degrees. The continuous loop blade cuts quietly and efficiently, creating less noise, less waste, and less dust than a table saw.

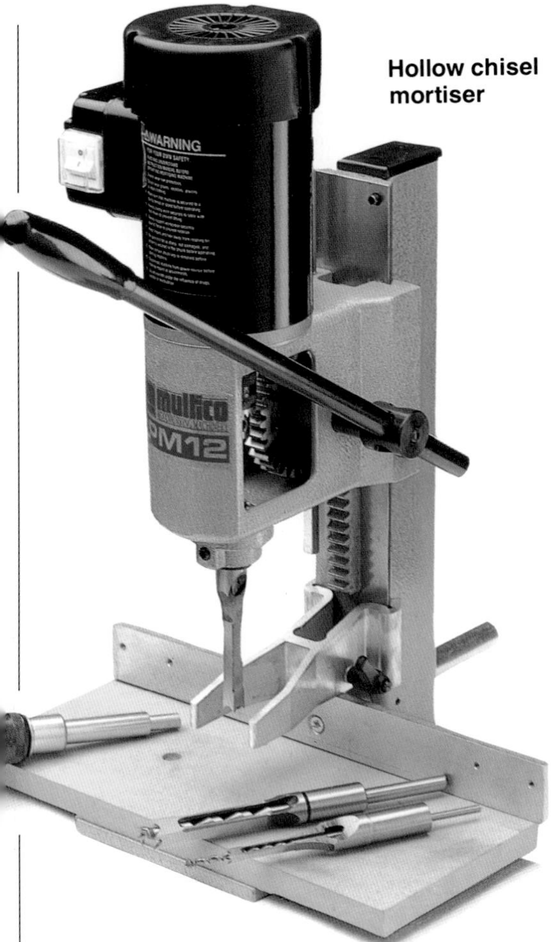

Hollow chisel mortiser

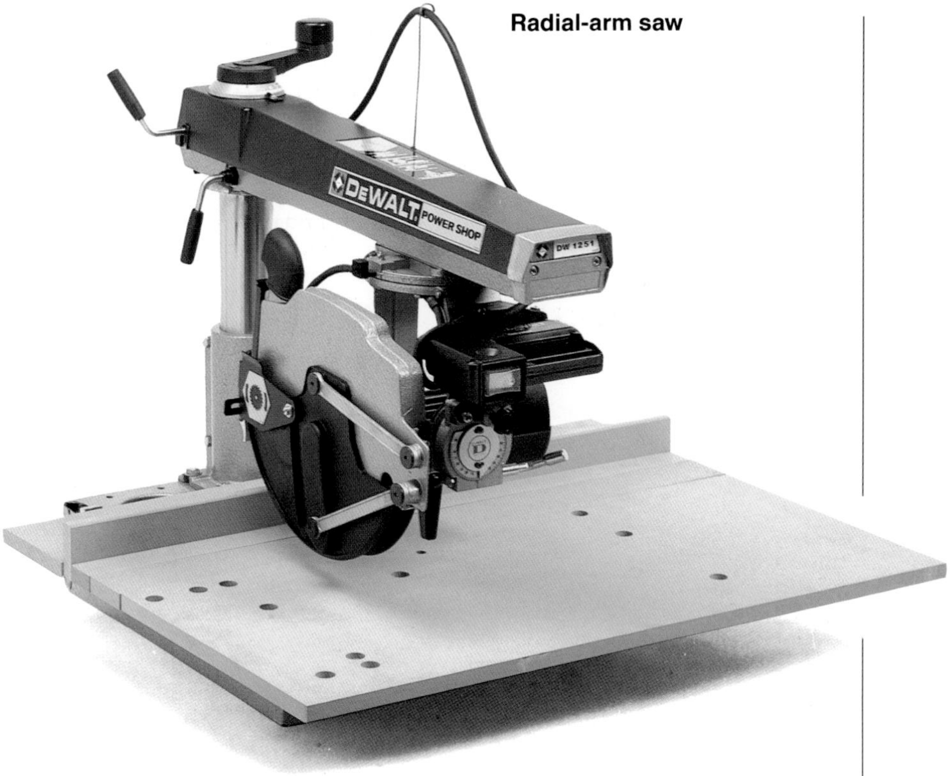

Radial-arm saw

▲The radial-arm saw is a highly versatile machine that is capable, among other actions, of cross-cutting, ripping, and grooving wood.

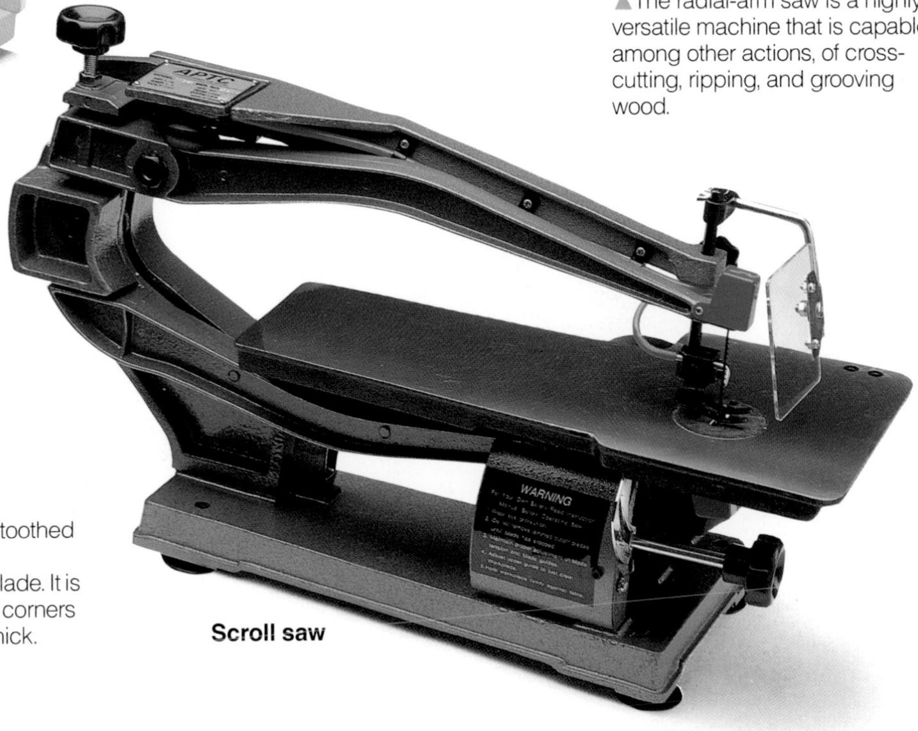

▲The hollow chisel mortiser combines the pressing action of a sharp-edged chisel with a drill-bit, which rotates within the "hollow" chisel to give a fast and effective way of cutting square slots in a piece of wood. Mortises of any width can be achieved by moving the piece along for each cut.

▶The scroll saw is a fine-toothed reciprocating saw with an inexpensive, disposable blade. It is used for cutting fine, tight corners in materials up to 1 inch thick.

Scroll saw

Planer-thicknesser

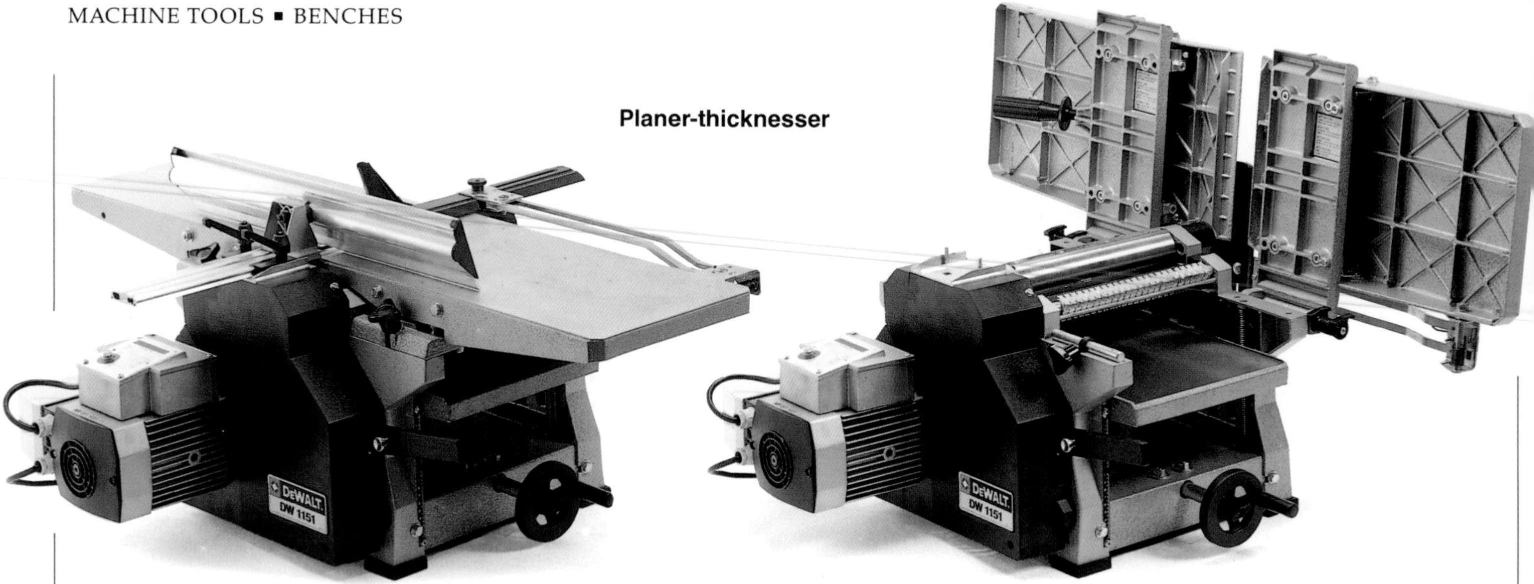

▲The planer-thicknesser, as its name suggests, combines the actions of planer and thicknesser. It can be used to plane the wood to create a flat surface and then, using the fence, to square the edges. As a thicknesser, it enables the wood to be machined parallel to the already dressed surfaces by means of an automatic feed. In some models, the surfacing table swings clear when the thicknesser action is in use.

▼The woodturning lathe is one of the simplest machine tools, and it has the additional advantage that complete objects can be made on it. The wood is precut into a more or less circular shape, mounted on the lathe – either on a faceplate or between centers – and spun at speed. A gouge or scraper against a tool rest is fed against the revolving wood.

Woodturning lathe

BENCHES

The woodworker's bench is the center of the workshop, from where all creativity springs. A bench should be sturdy and level, and at a height that suits you. It offers a flat, supporting surface, but should also include a vice and "dogs" to hold work. The best benches are made of seasoned beech, but you can improvise and build your own from reclaimed lumber. Above all, a bench should withstand the wrenching or shuddering caused by vigorous PLANING in the vice, when you put your entire weight behind the plane. Apart from the traditional bench, there are numerous ingenious folding and lightweight devices that grip wood in a variety of ways.

▶ This folding bench is a superbly designed device, which takes up little room when it is not needed, but which can grip or support awkwardly shaped work in its double vice jaw top and plastic "dogs." Extra support can be achieved when planing if you place one foot on the "step." The bench's versatility extends to gripping circular sections of wood of large and small diameters. However, its lightweight construction means that it is not designed to take a pounding from a mallet.

Portable folding bench or "Workmate"

The workbench
The classic European workbench. This model has a slot along the back edge in which to store tools, and a shelf beneath the top to hold pieces of wood and large items of equipment. This sturdy worktop is made of beech (in North America benchtops are traditionally in maple). The continental-style wooden vices grip firmly without marking the wood.

WOODS

Of the many thousands of woods known to be in existence, only a very small proportion is available commercially; of these no more than about 70 species could be said to be easy to come by. This is a situation which is likely to get more acute because of attitudes toward commercial harvesting in the rainforests.

Nevertheless, there is still a large choice available, and very often there are several species which may be equally suitable for the job at hand; a table for example may look just as good in oak as in elm and serve exactly the same purpose.

Buying wood

There are many ways in which wood can be bought, all of which in some way affects its price. The cheapest method is to buy "in the log," straight from the forest or lumber yard as a tree trunk. If you have the means to convert it, this is fine, but there are disadvantages; the most obvious being the uncertainty of the quality of the heartwood, which might have a disappointing grain or color, or may even be rotten.

Buying sawn boards is safer because the quality can be easily seen as the wood lies "stickered" – that is, stacked one board above the other with small battens in between to allow air flow for drying.

The next step is to get your local mill to convert it to the sizes you want and this is known as buying "rough-sawn." Many lumber yards stock rough-sawn lumber in a range of standard sizes and this is the bulk of the trade.

For the woodworker without a well-equipped workshop, the easiest way is to buy "prepared" wood which is "planed all around" on all four sides, and can very often be bought cut to length. Having passed through so many processes, this method of buying is obviously the most expensive.

What to look for

What to look for depends on what you want. You may want a good figure on oak, for example, or be looking for heavy contrasts in the color of walnut. Sometimes it may be necessary to purchase a whole board in order to get the small section that you want.

Generally speaking, good straight-grained, clean wood free from knots is desirable, but look for signs of warping. Heavy "shakes" (splits) in a large oak beam may be acceptable, but in a piece of pine or mahogany for cabinetwork they are most unwelcome.

Types of wood

There are three ways in which wood is classified: trade name; local name; or botanical name. The last of these is the only really safe one for identification. Generally you can rely on the trade name, but if you have any doubt, find out the botanical name. The main reason to know what you are buying is to make sure that the wood is suitable for its purpose. There are many hardwoods now on the market which were not exploited years ago and were introduced into the trade as substitutes for teak or mahogany and sold off as the real thing. Often they have similar properties, but it's worth checking, especially if you are buying in quantity.

Hardwoods and softwoods

This classification is something of a misnomer. Yew for example is a softwood, but it is extremely hard and can be difficult to work. Balsa is a hardwood and is very soft and can be cut and worked easily.

Hardwood refers to wood which comes from deciduous trees; softwoods come from coniferous trees. This is all that the terms mean; they have nothing to do with the properties of the wood itself.

Storage before use

For the cabinet maker, movement in wood can be a great problem, especially in the modern home environment with central heating. It is often difficult to know the moisture content of wood when it is first purchased, and without care, a beautifully crafted piece of furniture may shrink and open up after a few months in a heated atmosphere. You should try always to store your wood for some weeks in the environment in which the finished piece of furniture is going to be kept before starting work; if possible keep it in the house itself. Obviously this is not always possible, but care in storage does pay dividends. The following woods shown are a small but representative selection of those in fairly common use.

CEDAR OF LEBANON *softwood*
Characteristics A fine-textured resinous and sweet-smelling wood, usually fairly straight grained; poor bending qualities and low resistance to shock.
Uses Exterior work, greenhouses, garden furniture, light joinery.

PINE *softwood*
Characteristics Pale creamy yellow usually straight grained and often knotty; generally fine or medium textured; works and glues well; low resistance to shock.
Uses Very commonly used in joinery, doors, window frames etc; good source of turpentine and pitch.

ENGLISH YEW *softwood*
Characteristics Heavy lustrous wood with rich contrasts in color from pale cream to brown and purple; bends well, finishes well, close, even grain.
Uses Longbows, small turnings such as lace bobbins and bowls, marquetry inlays, veneers.

EUROPEAN LARCH *softwood*
Characteristics Straight-grained, pale reddish-brown heartwood, resinous and sometimes knotty; uniform texture; a tough wood that bends well and will take impact.
Uses Telegraph poles, boat planking, general joinery, pit props, veneers.

SCOTS PINE *softwood*
Characteristics Pale reddish-brown, resinous and with clearly defined annular rings; troublesome in gluing due to high resin content; works well; low resistance to shock.
Uses Building construction, piles, pit props, joinery, etc., veneers.

AMERICAN WHITE ASH *hardwood*
Characteristics Grayish-brown occasionally with a red cast; fairly coarse texture but generally even; bends well; stiff and strong with a good resistance to shock.
Uses A much used wood for handles such as in sports equipment, axs, garden tools, car bodies, joinery.

EUROPEAN BEECH *hardwood*
Characteristics Pinkish-brown and very pale, will turn darker with steaming, occasionally with dark veins; texture fine, even, and straight; bends exceptionally well and will glue easily; drill for nailing.
Uses Cabinet making, high-class joinery, tool handles, turning.

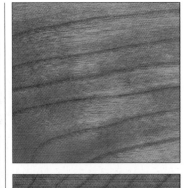

AMERICAN CHERRY *hardwood*
Characteristics Fine, close and straight-grained wood, reddish-brown and often flecked; a medium-strength wood which bends well and glues well; polishes to a high finish.
Uses Cabinet making, boat interiors, turning, inlay.

AMERICAN RED ELM *hardwood*
Characteristics Heavily marked with dark red stripes, works and bends exceptionally well; high resistance to shock loads; texture can be coarse, but usually acceptable; glues and nails easily.
Uses Vehicle bodies, boatbuilding, wheel hubs, turning, veneers.

BRAZILIAN MAHOGANY *hardwood*
Characteristics Light reddish-brown to beautiful rich red; coarse to medium grain can be interlocked, often straight; not really suitable for bending; easy to glue, nail, stain, and polish.
Uses Cabinet making, paneling, high-class furniture, boats, veneers.

FIGURED MYRTLE *hardwood*
Characteristics Anything from warm brown to yellow, maybe with a green tinge; texture firm and smooth; grain straight or irregular. A heavy wood with hard-wearing qualities.
Uses Paneling, flooring, turning, joinery, cabinet making, marquetry.

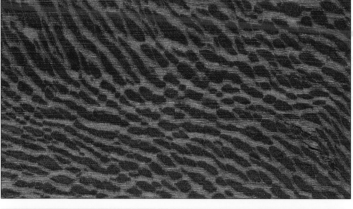

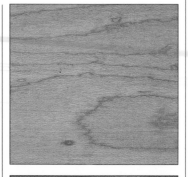

AMERICAN WHITE OAK *hardwood*
Characteristics Pale yellow to pink, normally straight grained with a figure on the quarter sawn; medium to coarse textured and light in weight; medium-crushing strength, bends well.
Uses Joinery, cabinet making, flooring, ladders, coffins, cooperage, paneling, veneers.

LONDON PLANE/LACEWOOD *hardwood*
Characteristics Reddish-brown, fairly light, very marked decorative rays on quarter sawn; medium texture, straight grain, sometimes fine; bends well and has medium strength.
Uses Turning, cabinet making, joinery; highly prized for inlays and veneers; useful for paneling and light carcassing.

AMERICAN MAPLE *hardwood*
Characteristics Creamy white to soft brown, straight grained, occasionally with flecks; bends reasonably well; medium strength in both bending and resistance to shock; nails, stains, and polishes well; moderate gluing potential.
Uses Cabinet making, joinery, flooring, turning, paneling.

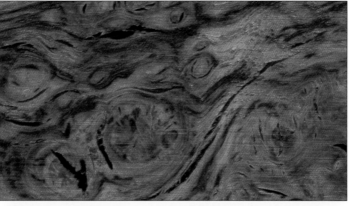

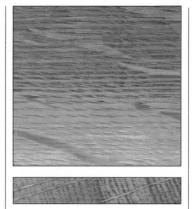

AMERICAN RED OAK *hardwood*
Characteristics Pinkish color, possibly reddish; coarse, straight grain not highly figured; medium-bending strength but bends well; crushing strength high.
Uses Interior joinery, furniture, flooring, plywood, veneers.

BURL OAK *hardwood*
Characteristics Like all burls, highly figured and visually exciting, virtually useless as a structural wood, but prized by turners and marqueters; spotted and warty in appearance.
Uses Turning, marquetry, inlay, and general decorative purposes.

ENGLISH OAK *hardwood*
Characteristics Biscuit colored or light brown, grain unpredictable, often straight, can be heavily interlocked; quarter sawn has distinctive rays; bends well but liable to stain if in contact with ferrous metals.
Uses Cooperage, boats, furniture, flooring, veneers.

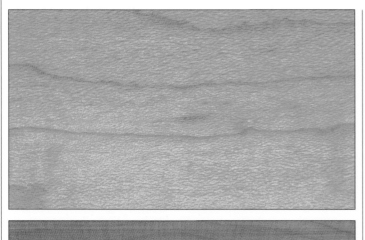

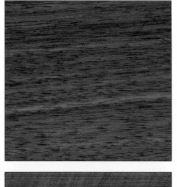

ROCK MAPLE *hardwood*
Characteristics White/creamy red, occasionally brown; variable grain from curly to straight; an even-textured wood with fine grain, bends well and retains high-strength characteristics; polishes, stains, and glues reasonably well.
Uses Turning, musical instruments, paneling, cabinet making, plywood.

AMERICAN BLACK WALNUT *hardwood*
Characteristics Dark brown to muddy purple, mainly straight grained but with some curls; a dense, hard wood with a coarse grain, bends well; screws and nails well.
Uses Interior joinery, quality furniture, carving, turning, veneers.

FRENCH WALNUT *hardwood*
Characteristics Brownish-gray, sometimes darker, often streaky; irregular grain with a medium to coarse texture; bends reasonably well, average resistance to shock; takes a high finish.
Uses A first-rate cabinet wood, also for gunstocks, doors, carving and turning, paneling, marquetry.

MANMADE BOARDS

Much of the ordinary household furniture bought today is manufactured from manmade boards such as plywood, particle board, and MDF. There are several reasons for this. First, it's cheap; second, it is often veneered with highly expensive woods which in the solid are not available; and third, because manmade boards come in large widths, they are very stable and will give no trouble in a warm, dry, centrally heated environment.

Manmade boards can also be environmentally friendly, in that they are often comprised of waste products from the mills, such as sawdust, bark, and cutoffs.

They are usually bonded with a resin which ties the particles together but has a devastating effect on tools unless they are tungsten-carbide tipped.

The cheapest of manmade boards, as far as the woodworker is concerned, is particle board, which is made from bonded wood chips. It's ideal for cladding, cheap carcassing, and for making forms and templates for more exacting work.

Plywood is ideal for kitchen countertops, boatbuilding (marine ply) as well as shuttering, general cladding applications, toymaking, and molds and forms.

For really good dimensional stability MDF is probably the best. It will take veneer well and is very easy to work with in the field of furniture making.

There are many types, grades, and thicknesses of manmade boards, and all have very useful applications in modern woodworking.

MDF
MDF is a relatively new material already proven in furniture, making and notable for its ability to work well and hold a fine edge.

Types of manmade boards
Left to right: masonite, three-ply board, three-layer particle board, plywood, MDF, birch multi-ply. Availability in large sizes is probably the greatest single selling point manmade boards have. This, coupled with worldwide availability, has made them indispensable in the last 40 years.

VENEERS AND INLAYS

Fine cabinetwork, boxmaking, and musical instruments have for hundreds of years been enhanced by veneers and inlays. These are their main applications and, when well done, veneering is a technique which has been the benchmark of real quality. It also gives woodworkers nowadays a chance to use rare woods otherwise out of reach.

A range of bandings
These long patterned strips can be used with veneers or they can be placed in shallow grooves in solid timber, either as a decorative border or in a geometric or other patterned form.

▶ Types of veneer
From left to right: aspen, Brazilian rosewood, olive ash, tropical olive, pomelle, pine, zebrano, cherry.

◀ A selection of marquetry motifs
These paper-backed, ready-made motifs are for use in marquetry projects.

Most wooden constructions combine several techniques. When you are making a table, for example, the wood has to be selected and squared, and then the joints are marked out, sawn, chiseled, and planed. The piece has to be glued and clamped, and finally finished.

The following encyclopedia section uses step-by-step demonstrations to explain these and many other basic techniques. The section is arranged alphabetically, and hand- and power-tool options are offered for each technique. Cross-references in the text will allow you quickly to build up your knowledge and, thus, your confidence. Each technique entry includes a checklist of essential equipment and a choice of items for hand- or power-tool enthusiasts.

TECHNIQUES

ABRADING

Abrading is the general term applied to smoothing wood before applying a FINISH, but it is also a term for shaping wood using hand or power tools. Although much abrading does consist of sanding for a fine finish, it would be limiting to confine the term to this function only, since abrading is also a very important shaping technique. There are many instances, which you will no doubt come across, when other tools cannot easily fashion the wood. For example, in instances when chisels or planes might split the grain or when a saw is used to cut out the desired profile roughly, the general shaping and finishing is done by abrading.

Abrading involves the wearing away of wood fibers by the multiple sharp-toothed action of an abrasive material such as sandpaper. It also refers to the action of files or rasps and specific power tools and their accessories.

In some instances both hand- and power-tool abrading methods can be used, although the latter is generally quicker and more efficient.

At the heart of most abrading is sandpaper, usually a sheet or roll onto which the abrasive particles are bonded. The particle sizes are graded as a "grit," and these are numbered. Generally you work through the grades, starting with a coarser grit and going through to the finer ones until the wood is smooth and there are no visible sanding marks.

CHECKLIST

A range of sandpapers
Soft blanket or cloth for protecting work when finishing
———
Cork sanding block
A range of workshop-made sanding sticks
———
Disk-sanding table attachment
Power drill, 550 watts.
Orbital sander
Belt sander
———
See pages 8-9

TYPES OF ABRASIVE

SANDPAPER
Flint paper Useful in carpentry/joinery for general finishing.

Garnet paper Preferred by cabinetmakers and fine woodworkers because of its excellent finishing properties.

Aluminum oxide A good all-round sandpaper and particularly used in powered sanding.

Silicon carbide Mainly for metal, but useful on some hard lacquers and finishes used on furniture.

STEEL WOOL
Main grades used in woodwork are No.1, No.0, No.00, and No.000. Mainly used for smoothing down between sanding or for the application of wax in the finishing process.

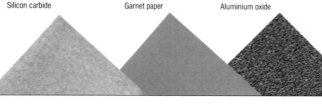

Silicon carbide   Garnet paper   Aluminium oxide

Hand sanding – shaping with an abrasive stick

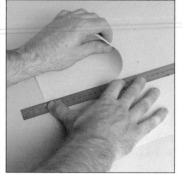

1 Tear off strips of sandpaper to the required size using a steel ruler. Tearing "freehand" is messy and wasteful.

2 Wrap the sandpaper around a workshop-made wood forming block, creasing the edges back on themselves to form a sharp edge which clings to the block.

Sanding Chart

grade	grit		applications
very coarse	50	1	heavy shaping
	60	1/2	
coarse	80	0	shaping – belt, disk, orbital and hand
	100	2/0	
medium	120	3/0	shaping and finishing – belt, disk, orbital and hand sanding
	150	4/0	
	180	5/0	
fine	220	6/0	finishing – power and hand sanding
	240	7/0	
	280	8/0	
very fine	320	9/0	final finishing, taking off sharp edges, sanding between coats of lacquer – hand sanding
	360		
	400		
	500		
	600		

3 Hold the work in the vice and use the sanding block or stick like a file, preferably with both hands, cutting across the fibers. Change the sanding strips when they begin to lose their bite and clog up with waste (especially when sanding resinous woods).

4 You can easily make different profile blocks or sticks to sand curves and angled profiles. Improvised materials such as a short length of plastic pipe can serve as an accurate former for concave sanding. You can use it like a file with fingers at each end to help stabilize the action which goes across the grain, weakening the fibers.

5 The sanding stick method is very versatile. Here one hand sands while the other hand rotates the work.

6 You can work a thin strip of coarse sandpaper "bath towel" fashion to form circular sections accurately.

Using a hand-block

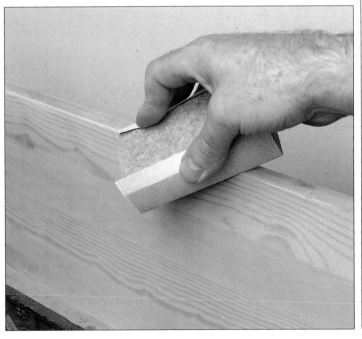

1 A cork hand-block is normally used for flat work. Mount the paper on the block, secure the work in the vice or on the bench, and apply firm pressure, working along the grain. More pressure and control can be achieved with both hands on the block. Use 120–180 grit paper.

2 When the grain runs the other way, try to sand with the grain; otherwise, scratch marks will show.

3 Generally speaking, wooden objects should not be left with sharp edges. A final finishing procedure is to "soften" all edges with fine sandpaper (400 grit).

Power sanding – shaping

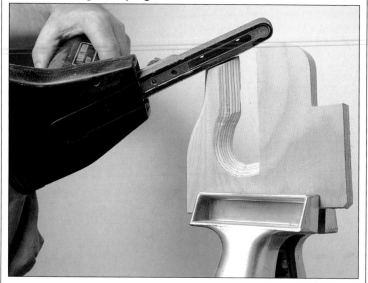

This narrow-belt power sanding tool can fashion wood fast and furiously. First secure the work in the vice. The tool needs firm control directed at its tip where it generally does the work.

Shaping and finishing using a power sander

1 A disk-sanding table attachment for a power drill is useful and accurate for angled or curved end grain sanding. Ensure the work is fed into the rotation of the disk. This means that the rotation of the disk should push the work downward onto the bench and not try to flip it up.

2 The table can be angled upward and a bevel fence used on its face as a guide for compound angles. This is where an angle runs off at two planes rather than one.

Using a belt sander

1 A belt sander has a continuous 3- or 4-inch-wide belt passing over a flat bed via two rollers.
It abrades faster than other power sanders, and the tool has to be held firmly to keep it from snatching and taking off.

2 The belt is changed quickly by a release lever which slackens the tension. Tracking is adjusted by a knob.

3 A belt sander can be inverted for flat and curved sanding. Ensure it is clamped to the bench and the work held firmly as it is fed into the sander.

Using an orbital sander

An orbital sander is ideal for sanding large panels flat. Sanding sheets are attached to the cushioned oscillating baseplate. Let the weight of the tool do most of the work, and keep moving it up and down and across the work in gentle sweeping actions.

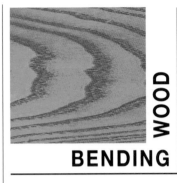

BENDING WOOD

A natural characteristic of wood is that it bends. This is what inspired the great Finnish architect Alvar Aalto. Some woods, however, are more bendy than others. Ash, beech, and yew, for example, yield more easily than mahogany or teak. This section looks at ways in which you can bend wood which, in turn, will open up enormous creative possibilities.

A thin-cut section of wood bends more easily than a thick section, and when it is wet or hot, it is even more pliable. Bending is an economic way to fashion the material because forming curves by jointing straight pieces and then shaping them (see SHAPING WOOD) is more complex, time consuming, and wasteful of material.

Wood bending is a technique often used in Scandinavian furniture, resulting in beautifully understated pieces which are light and strong with an integrity of structure and form.

The main wood-bending techniques are: steam bending, laminating, and saw kerfing (although saw kerfing offers very little strength because most of the fibers are cut through).

It is also possible to bend wood using microwave technology, which can be easily done with a home microwave oven although, because of the restriction of size, the method is most suited to modelmaking or shaping inlay strips (see VENEERING).

There is no doubt that bends or curves in furniture are pleasing to the eye, and with a little imagination and improvisation you can make your own bending jigs. You can apply the method to all sorts of household items from salad servers and clock cases to chair backs or even complete chairs.

Saw kerfing

Saw kerfing is the least strong of all the bending methods. In fact, because the wood is all but cut through its entire thickness, it offers very little strength and would only be suitable for non-load bearing applications such as bases with curved corners.

Sometimes two saw kerfed bends can be glued together with the saw cuts facing in, but generally, care has to be taken not to split the fibers when bending away from the saw cuts.

The method can be achieved with a handsaw and jig, or with a bandsaw against a stop, and the most quick and efficient method is with a radial-arm saw.

Radial-arm saw kerfing

1 A strip of narrow board is cut to size (see SQUARING WOOD) and mounted on the radial-arm saw table against the fence. Place a pencil or ballpoint pen mark on the fence about ³⁄₈ inch from the saw-blade cut. This is the spaced distance between saw kerfs.

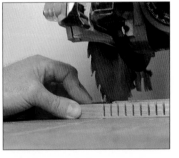

2 Set the radial-arm saw-blade height just short of cutting all the way through the wood. Draw the saw across and make a series of cuts, moving the wood each time and aligning the previous cut with the mark. The depth of cut may need adjusting to get the required bend. You can see how effective this simple method is, but remember the saw cuts have taken the strength out of the wood.

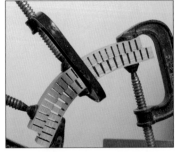

3 By gluing and clamping two saw-kerf bends with their cuts inward, you can create an interesting structure, albeit with limited strength in certain applications (see VENEERING).

Laminating

Numerous thin strips or laminations of wood – up to ⅛ inch thick – are cut and then glued together and bent around a form, usually a male and female mold. The terms male and female, when applied to molds, refer to convex and concave shapes which usually match

The grain follows the length of the strips, and the use of a synthetic glue makes a very strong bond.

The method is suited to mass production as the machining and gluing is automated. Highly precise stainless-steel hydraulically operated molds are used in conjunction with rapid microwave glue curing.

Low-cost individual laminating can be achieved by sawing thin strips and forming them in a particle-board male and female form. However, sawing does produce some waste as the saw kerf can almost be as thick as the laminate.

It is important to leave the glue to cure overnight before taking the wood out of the form.

Laminating

1 Construct a male and female mold, allowing for the thickness of the entire laminated structure, which means the curves follow two different radii. Cut some laminates (see SAWING) ⅛ inch thick in ash or beech, and mix some plastic resin and apply to each laminate. The laminates are clamped in the male and female form using a bar or quick-release clamp to close them up.

2 "C" clamps are now added to pull the form in tightly. This jig demonstrates a simple radius, but of course other curved forms can be achieved. This is the basic principle of structural wood laminating, and the resulting structures are very strong. A plastic sheathing has been used here to prevent the laminates from becoming stuck to the form. After the laminates have fully cured, the edges are trimmed with a plane.

Laminating using veneers

 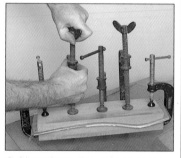

1 Usually beech constructional veneer is used with a more decorative facing veneer. Constructional veneers are thicker than normal veneers. The bends can be fairly tight because the veneer is pliable. In this simple form, a thin protective plastic sheet is used to prevent glue sticking to the form. Apply a thin coat of glue on one side of the veneers.

2 Now clamp the veneers in the form with "C" clamps, taking care to align the male and female parts of the form perfectly. The laminated veneers are left to cure overnight in a warm place.

Steam bending

Steam bending involves putting the wood in a sealed chamber which is filled with steam from a constant source; on a small scale this can be a stove kettle. When it is fully saturated, the wood is taken out and bent with force around a shaped form.

The method is somewhat "hit or miss" as the final bend may straighten out slightly when dry, and bends which are too tight can break. It is rare for wood thicker than about 1⅜ inches to be steam bent, although 2 inches has been achieved in some industrial production such as the seats of the classic Thonet chairs.

Even then, a percentage of the tight bends break in the process.

Steam bending is particularly suited to home-workshop low-cost improvisation.

Steam bending

1 Build a form using plywood, particle board, or MDF to the desired shape and thickness. You can cut large holes to accommodate "C" clamps. Make a bending strap from thin sheet steel, and anchor it into the handles with bolts and screws.

2 For steaming the wood, you will need a steam generator, such as a pressure cooker shown here, and a steam chamber, which can be a plywood box or piece of plastic drainpipe plugged at both ends with wooden disks. Into one end a tube enters carrying a constant source of steam. It is important to insulate the steam chamber to keep the temperature as high as possible. Here the drainpipe is insulated with aluminum foil and fiberglass roof insulation.

3 Wooden plugs are made for the ends of the steam chamber, which is mounted at a slight downward slant so condensed water can escape at the end into a bucket.

4 At the feed end (with its plug removed) the wood is stacked on spacers ready for steaming. Replace the plug with the hose entering it. Switch on the steam generator controlling the heat setting, so that a constant supply of steam passes through the chamber (escaping from the drainhole at the other end). As a rule of thumb, three-quarters of an hour is needed for every 1 inch thickness of wood to be bent.

 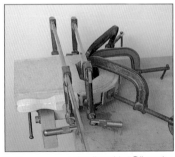  

Microwave bending

5 After the wood has been steamed, you must quickly transfer it to the bending jig, strap it in, and make the bend at once. Some trial and error is required to get it right. The steel strap helps prevent fiber break-out.

6 Now secure the jig with "C" and bar clamps and allow to dry for several days.

1 A microwave oven can be used to heat small sections of wood enough for subsequent bending and forming in male and female molds. The method takes some experimenting with.

2 It helps to keep the wood moist by wrapping it in a stout, sealed plastic bag with a little water in it or wrapping it in a saturated cloth. The microwave oven is set at its "high" position and timed for 3–5 minutes for a bend of about ⅛-inch thickness. After microwaving, the wood is quickly placed in the form and clamped together and left for a few hours to fully dry out.

JOINTS

BISCUIT

Biscuit jointing is a modern method of wood jointing which you can use as an alternative to many traditional joints. It is a quick and easy jointing system suitable for carcasses and frames in solid wood and manufactured board.

The biscuit joint combines a simple butt or miter joint with an elliptical compressed wood insert called a biscuit which gives the joint its strength. The biscuit slot is easily located and cut with a biscuit jointer – a small diameter circular saw with a plunging cutter.

The tool consists of a spring-loaded cutter assembly/motor housing, a baseplate, and an adjustable guide fence with an additional bevel fence for inserting biscuits into miter joints. You can adjust the depth-of-cut to suit the biscuit, and the blade can also be finely adjusted horizontally.

The joint is very easily marked on the pieces of wood, and the biscuit jointer is positioned correctly and then plunged to make its cut. The biscuit itself is made of compressed beech and is available in three sizes. The entire joint is glued, usually with white or yellow glue (which is available under various names). The glue causes the biscuit to swell, so fairly quick assembly is advisable. For multiple biscuit joints, a slower-working glue should be used, such as a plastic resin glue.

Biscuit joints can never be as strong as traditional joints, such as the MORTISE-AND-TENON or DOVETAIL, but they are ideal for constructions such as small boxes, kitchen cupboards, and edge-jointing solid wood boards in which the joint serves as a locating system for keeping adjoining boards flush when gluing.

Spacing biscuit joints

The spacing of biscuit joints is not critical; every 2 or 3 inches is adequate. In thick-sectioned frames, the biscuits can be double-inserted across the thickness of the stock, but the joint should be used for center rails and not as a replacement for a mortise-and-tenon on corners of frames.

The biscuit jointer can also be used to cut grooves along the wood as a slot or locating point for other joints, as in modern drawer construction (see also JOINTS.)

CHECKLIST

Ballpoint pen/pencil
Ruler
Biscuit jointer
Hammer
Bar clamps
"C" clamps
White or yellow glue
or
Plastic resin glue
✛
See pages 8-9

Biscuit jointing a wide panel: "L" and "T" configurations

1 Prepare the ends of panels for jointing (butt joint), ensuring the joint surfaces are true and flat. You can handplane them or use them straight from the machine saw, but they must be accurate.

2 Mark the biscuit joint centers on the panels to be jointed, copying one from the other. For a "T" configuration, a squared line across the panel will help to position the adjacent member.

SOME APPLICATIONS FOR BISCUIT JOINTS

Biscuit joints are a versatile modern system which can be used to form joints in a variety of simple butt configurations.

Biscuit joints can be used to edge-joint narrow boards for use in making table tops or other wide surfaces.

A biscuit jointer can be used to join together the sides of a drawer and also to groove out for the base.

Double biscuit joints can be used on sturdy sections such as center rails where the load is not too excessive.

 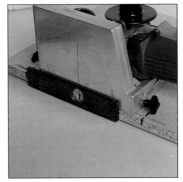 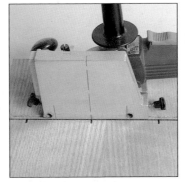 

3 Now secure the panel in the vice and set the tool for cutter depth, adjusting the fence so that the biscuit is central across the thickness of the panel. Align the tool with the marked position on the panel and carefully make a plunge cut. Then withdraw without disturbing the position. Repeat the action for multiple joints.

4 With the fence still attached to the biscuit jointer, position the tool at the end of the adjoining panel for an "L" joint and align it with the mark. Carefully make a plunge cut for the corresponding joint. Take your time doing this, and work slowly and deliberately.

5 For a "T" joint remove the fence from the tool and align the edge of the tool along the squared pencil line, positioning it to the biscuit center mark. Carefully plunge the tool to make the matching cut. Some biscuit jointers are heavier than others, and this may affect the "freehand" method. If you have difficulty, you can use double-sided tape on the base of the tool to help it grip.

6 Alternatively, "C" clamp a stop or another panel along the squared pencil line and butt the edge of the tool against it, and make the cuts to the biscuit center positions.

Making miter cuts

1 For maximum-strength MITER cuts, the fence has to be set so that the biscuit center is slightly nearer the inner face of the panel. Secure the panel in the vice and carefully plunge the tool at the marked positions on both pieces.

2 Alternatively the biscuit jointer's miter fence can be used in conjunction with the mitered edge of the other panel clamped securely and squarely to the workpiece. When cutting mitered joints with the miter fence, fine horizontal blade adjustment can be made. Note that there are numerous alignment marks on the baseplate.

3 Glue the joint together with white or yellow glue, using a thin wood strip to coat every surface. Remember that particle board absorbs glue, so be generous and work quickly. Drive the joint home with a hammer and scrapwood block, using bar clamps (see GLUING). If there is a lot of gluing to be done, then instead of white or yellow use a synthetic glue.

BUTT AND RABBET JOINTS

The butt joint is the simplest of corner joints (if it can be called a joint at all), as it consists of two square-ended pieces of wood meeting together without any overlap. Because of this, it needs reinforcement by gluing, nailing, or screwing. Glue alone will hold the joint together.

CHECKLIST

Marking gauge
Steel ruler
White or yellow glue
Brads, nails, or screws
———————
Tenon saw
Pencil
½-inch chisel
Mallet
Smoothing or jack plane
———————
Table disk sander and power drill
Radial-arm saw or small table saw
or small router
———————
See pages 8-9

However, it is not a very strong or permanent bond as the end grain absorbs much of the glue, and end grain gluing should generally be avoided in woodworking. Subsequent wood movement (shrinkage) can cause the joint to come apart over a period of time. A better reinforcement to the butt joint is to dowel it together (see DOWEL JOINTS).

The rabbet joint, which is a development of the butt joint, combines a butt on one piece and a stepped cut-out on the other. This gives slightly more mechanical integrity and a longer glue line for greater strength.

It also needs reinforcing with pins, which help to hold the wood together while gluing (see GLUING). Butt and rabbet joints are used for lightweight frames and carcasses of a joinery nature, and for small boxes where the top and base pieces add to the strength of the joint.

However, despite the simplicity of butt and rabbet joints, you will find they can be tricky to make. In fact when using hand tools, butt and rabbet joints involve one of the most difficult woodworking tasks – cutting the ends of the pieces of wood perfectly "square" (90 degrees) (see SQUARING WOOD).

This is made much easier by the use of an appropriate power tool such as a table saw, a radial-arm saw, or a bandsaw, finishing off to a line with a disk sander.

Making a rabbet joint using hand tools

1 First prepare both pieces of wood to size (see SQUARING WOOD), paying particular attention to squaring off the ends of both pieces of wood. It is good practice to use a plane with a scrapwood block at the back of the work to prevent the wood from splitting. Work to a cut line and check the result with a try square.

2 Set a marking gauge to the thickness of the wood and gauge a line on the face of the lapping piece. Then extend the lines on the edges to about two-thirds the thickness of the wood and reset the gauge to mark a narrow line along the end of the piece, extending it along the edges to meet up with the first line.

COMMON USES

If additional strength is required, butt and rabbets can either be screwed or nailed together into the end grain.

Butt and rabbet joints can be used for right-angle or "T" connections in areas where no great strength is required in the joint.

Butt joints help with the alignment and assembly of frames and carcasses. In the latter, extra strength is gained when the top and base members are attached.

3 With a pencil, shade in the waste to be cut away. This clearly shows which portion of the wood is to be removed. Place the wood in the vice and use a tenon saw to cut down the grain, always working on the waste side of the line (see SAWING).

4 If you now place the wood in the vice at a slight angle, you can either saw across the grain to the line or remove the portion of waste with a chisel by cutting either with the grain or across it (see CHISELING).

5 Assuming the rabbet joint is part of a framework or small carcass, apply glue to the joints and assemble, using either pins, clamps, or masking tape to pull the joints together.

Making a rabbet joint using power tools

2 Another quick method you might like to try is to clamp the piece to the bench and use the ROUTER. Set this up with a straight bit and fence to rout out the stepped portion.

1 Power tools are a much faster method of making rabbet joints. After squaring the wood, place two marks on the end of the piece to show the depth and width you will work to using a radial-arm saw. Pull the saw back to make a series of cuts. For cutting multiple joints, a stop can be fixed for instant location of the work points. This can save you a lot of time.

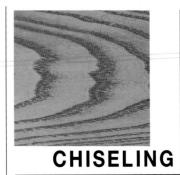

CHISELING

Like sawing, chiseling is an essential woodworking skill. It is primarily a hand technique requiring some degree of dexterity, which with practice you will soon acquire. The hand chisel is used for cutting, trimming, and shaping, and in particular for removing stock or waste in joint cutting.

Powered chiseling (mortising) generally refers to the use of a purpose-built hollow-chisel mortiser or an attachment to the power drill which cuts rectangular slots out of the wood. It combines the action of an auger drill and a square-edged chisel, which is pressed with force into the work. In general this method is found more in industrial workshops, and the powered mortiser is

certainly not a necessity for the home hobbiest. This method is usually applied to cutting mortises (see MORTISE-AND-TENON JOINTS).

Common to all chiseling is the design of the chisel blade. This is beveled or sloped to a razor-sharp edge which has to be kept sharp (see TOOL MAINTENANCE).

There are two bevels: the ground angle (approximately 25 degrees), in which condition the tool is normally bought; and the sharpened angle (approximately 30 degrees). The sharpened angle is put on using an oilstone or something similar in your own workshop. Chisels do vary in action, and a shallower ground or sharpened blade slices through the wood more easily than a steeper-angled chisel, although the latter is stronger. Types of chisels vary from bevel-edged (which in this case means that the sides of the chisel are sloped also, but not sharpened); firmer (square-edged for some joint cutting); and mortise chisels (which are stouter and can be leveraged in and out of the wood).

Hand chiseling takes some practice, but done well, it is very rewarding.

Working across the grain

1 The chisel can be used efficiently to sever fibers across the grain; a little help with a mallet is needed here. A general rule is that when cutting a mortise, or similar square recess, the fibers are cut across the grain first to prevent splitting.

2 After the fibers have been severed across the grain, you can then chisel down the grain without splitting the fibers. A series of cuts to loosen the fibers precedes the final cut to the line.

Narrow chisels vs wide chisels

3 With both hands behind the chisel's cutting edge, one hand is used to deliver the power and the other to guide the chisel. The guiding hand is crucial for control, and here the fingers squeeze tightly around the chisel blade and the index finger rests against the edge of the work, acting as a depth-stop.

Experience will show that more cutting control is achieved with a narrow chisel than with a wide one, as there is less resistance from the wood fibers. Chisels vary in width from about ⅛ inch to 1½ inches. A bevel-edged ⅜ or ½ inch chisel is a good size to use for general work.

Working along the grain

1 The fibrous nature of wood lends itself to the action of the chisel, which by its wedge-shaped section slices into the wood, separating the fibers along the grain. Hold the chisel firmly, with both hands behind the cutting edge.

2 Here the chisel is held like a dagger for overhead paring, which means cutting along the grain. The guiding fingers and thumb give excellent control for taking off the exact amount of wood. The chisel is frequently used in conjunction with the saw, and here the saw has been used to sever the fibers across the grain first.

3 Alternatively you can chisel away the waste by holding the wood horizontally. Depending on the grain character of the wood, you might find it easier to cut across the grain first and then finish to the line with the grain, or vice versa! It depends on how the grain wants to behave. In any event, you should always work to a marked line.

Forming curves

Although there are quicker ways to form curves (see SHAPING WOOD), the chisel can be used to radius (curve) a corner, paring a series of fine flat cuts.

Using a mortise chisel

1 The mortise chisel is strong enough to lever against the wood, helping with the removal of chips.

2 A series of cuts across the grain breaks the wood up into small chips. You will find these are easy to remove when cutting a typical feature such as a hinge recess (see HINGES AND LOCKS).

Powered chiseling (mortising)

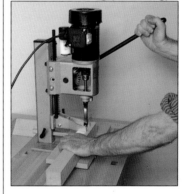

1 A hollow chisel mortiser is easy to use once the work has been aligned and clamped. Be sure to spend time in getting this right; it is a very important part of the job.

2 A series of square holes is cut to make a mortise. The auger bit cuts a hole, and the square-bodied, sharp-edged chisel housing is pressed into the wood, making a clean square-edged cut.

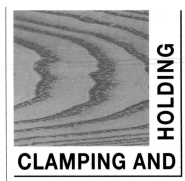

CLAMPING AND HOLDING

The need to hold work securely is important in woodworking. If the wood itself isn't secured, you will not be able to operate tools efficiently and safely. For example, no matter how steady your hand is at sawing, if the wood is not held firmly, the saw will jam in the cut. This leads to frustration, unsatisfactory results, and possibly injury. There are also times when just one pair of hands is not enough, and improvised holding devices are needed. As you progress in woodworking, you will probably find that you can make your own, to suit your own needs.

CHECKLIST

Woodworking bench
Bench-hook
Woodworkers' vice
"C" or "quick-release" clamps
Long "quick-release" or bar clamps
Glue gun and glue sticks
Bench stops
Double-sided tape
✛
See pages 8-9

The woodworking bench

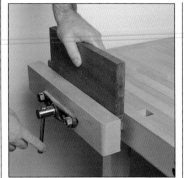

Apart from being a firm and solid base, the woodworking bench is the most basic holding and supporting device. Incorporated into it is usually a metal or wooden vice which supports work up to about 6 inches wide. Metal vices should be faced with sturdy hardwood. This is to prevent bruising the wood being held. Holes to secure the wooden faces are almost always pre-drilled by the manufacturers, and wooden faces are installed by the user.

As a general rule, keep the wood as low as possible in the vice to avoid vibration or "chatter" when sawing or planing.

Using a vice

1 The vice can hold work in a variety of ways, for instance, using the benchtop as extra support. For planing curves, short work can be gripped end-to-end. To plane, simply release the pressure and rotate the wood after each cut.

2 Awkward holding situations can be overcome by tilting the wood at an angle in the vice to give steady support for planing or sawing.

Using "C" and "quick-release" clamps

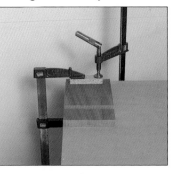

1 A variety of "C" or "quick-release" clamps is essential to a workshop kit. Two clamps on the bench can firmly support the work for chiseling, sawing, and drilling. Use scrapwood to prevent the clamp from damaging the wood.

2 Quick-release clamps combine the advantages of "C" clamps and bar clamps and are available in various lengths. They are suitable for holding work together during GLUING.

Using a bench-hook

A bench-hook (which can be easily made) is an excellent partner to the vice, and this will give you extra stability when sawing wood.

Using a bar clamp

To support long or extra wide work, the vice can accommodate a bar clamp with wood blocks. A bar clamp mounted in the vice is also particularly useful for planing long, square work to make it circular. This is done by planing away the sharp edges first from 4 to 8 (rotating as you go), then from 8 to 16 and so on, until the wood is round.

Using an end vice and dogs

If you hold thin wood in a vice, it may bow under the pressure; the benchtop is better because the wood can lie flat upon it. Therefore some workbenches include an end vice which operates with insertable dogs. These are pieces of wood or plastic which are inserted into pre-cut holes along the bench's length. The holes are spaced about 6 inches apart.

Using a bench stop

For planing thin wood, a bench stop can be improvised by using a "C" clamp to hold a thinner piece of plywood on the benchtop. Make sure it is large enough for the planing action not to hit the clamps.

Using folding workbenches

1 Modern universal folding workbenches incorporate plastic dogs which can hold virtually any shaped work. These cleverly designed devices can be very useful, especially when used for planing or sawing.

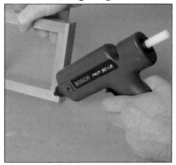

2 They can support circular sectioned work both horizontally and vertically.

The hot-melt glue gun

Use a hot-melt glue gun to hold wood in position temporarily. Apply glue "blobs" and allow to cool slightly on four points of the wood. Press the wood onto the workbench where it is ideally placed for routing operations when a vice or clamp might impede the router fence. The bond is only temporary, and the wood can be pried loose.

Using tape

Double-sided tape is remarkably strong for temporarily securing work to the bench, or for securing jig templates to the wood.

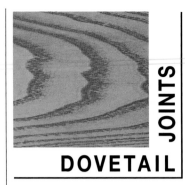

DOVETAIL JOINTS

No other woodworking joint has the universal appeal of the dovetail. It seems to express the whole spirit of wood crafts-manship yet, paradoxically, as a joint it is virtually redundant today in its strictest mechanical sense. There are other joints which, combined with the advantages of modern

CHECKLIST

Try square
Steel ruler
Marking knife
Pencil
Marking gauge
Dovetail scriber
Dovetail template or sliding bevel

———————

Dovetail saw
Coping saw
Bevel-edged chisel(s)
Mallet
Hammer and scrapwood
Handplane
Readymade dovetail jig

———————

Router (ideally 1300 watts plus)
Appropriate dovetail and straight bits
(tungsten-carbide tipped or
high-speed steel)

———————

See pages 8-9

"permanent" glues, are just as strong and a lot quicker to make.

Traditionally the dovetail was used by cabinetmakers in the fronts of drawers; the pull of the drawer acted against the wedged design of the joint, making it very strong. This is because the greater the pull on the handle, the tighter the joint became. The effect was to pull the joint together rather than apart. The dovetail will probably always hold great appeal, not just visually but as a challenge for woodworkers to make in its variety of forms. In hand woodworking it is commonly regarded as the last bastion of craftsmanship.

It can be made by hand or machine, and recent dovetail jigs involving the router (see ROUTING) now make the machine dovetail look as good as the traditional hand-cut version. There are various types of dovetail ranging from lap dovetails, secret-mitered dovetails, single dovetails, and common dovetails. All basically depend upon the same wedge shape to give them mechanical strength, so demonstrated here is the common dovetail as a useful illustration of the technique.

Laying out a common dovetail joint

1 After cutting the wood to size (see SQUARING WOOD), on each piece mark light shoulder lines all the way around to the thickness of the other piece plus $1/32$ inch. You can use a try square and marking knife, keeping the stock against the face marks.

2 Using a dovetail template and pencil, mark the positions of the dovetails on one piece. Always shade in the waste. The pitch angle is usually around 1:7 and can be marked alternatively with a sliding bevel. Pitch is the term used to denote the angle of the slope.

3 Using a try square, square the lines across the end of the wood and shade in the waste. This is very important so you know which parts to cut out.

Sawing the joint

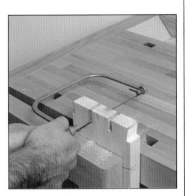

1 Secure the wood in the vice and tilt it at an angle so that you can saw the dovetails vertically. You will find this aids accurate cutting because gravity naturally pushes the saw down. Use a dovetail saw for fine work. It is crucial to saw on the waste side of the line leaving the entire line intact.

2 Using a try square and marking knife, deepen the shoulder line where the joint is to be cut.

3 Remove the end waste with a tenon saw, working down across the grain carefully to the line.

4 Remove the waste with a coping saw cutting to about ⅛ inch of the shoulder line. The ⅛ inch is left on at this stage because it can only be removed accurately with a very sharp chisel.

Chiseling the joint

1 Chisel back to the shoulder line using a bevel-edged chisel and mallet; use a series of fine vertical cuts to half the thickness of the wood. Then turn the wood around to cut from the other side. This will prevent the wood fibers from splitting or breaking out.

2 Finally clean up the shoulder lines with the chisel by mounting the wood back in the vice.

Transferring the marks

1 Now mount the second piece of wood in the vice at the raised level of a spacer piece, laid on the benchtop to ensure it lies flat, and carefully place the first piece (with tails cut) onto it. Align the shoulder lines and far edges perfectly. Mark the joint using a sharp pencil or dovetail scriber. Then shade in the waste.

2 Extend the vertical lines down the front of the joint using a try square. Now shade the waste wood using a series of clear diagonal lines. It makes cutting much easier.

Cutting the matching piece

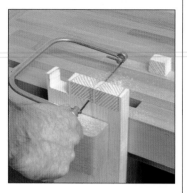

1 Carefully use a dovetail saw to cut on the waste side of the line down the grain to the shoulder line.

2 As before, a coping saw is used to remove the waste nearly to the line. Be careful not to cut into the angled pins.

Chiseling the matching piece

1 You can deepen the cut on the shoulder line to define it clearly for chiseling it back.

2 Carefully chisel back to the shoulder line overlapping each chisel cut to maintain a straight line. A narrow chisel gives much better control (see CHISELING).

Clamping

1 Clamp the dovetail joint together using a cut-out scrap block to allow the fingers to squeeze together up to the shoulder line. Using the scrap block prevents bruising from the clamp and also helps to spread the pressure from the clamp more evenly. Check that the joint is square with a try square (see GLUING).

2 After gluing, clean up the joint with a plane working inward to avoid splitting the end grain on the joint itself. The edges of the joint can be planed diagonally to tidy them up, holding the wood in the vice.

Using a jig to make a common dovetail joint

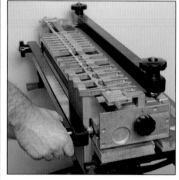

1 A particular jig was used in this demonstration – it shares some features with other jigs, other features are unique. If you do use a jig, first read the manufacturer's manual thoroughly to familiarize yourself with the particular type. Having read the manufacturer's manual, set up the jig and insert the wood for cutting the tails.

2 The positions of dovetails can be quickly set by tightening up the adjustable reversible fingers using the template in the "pins" mode.

Assembly and gluing

3 Now place the wood in the vice so that you can chisel horizontally to clean up the shoulder line. Take care not to cut right across, otherwise you will split the fibers.

4 Use a chisel to pare a fine bevel on the inside of the dovetails as a leading edge for pressing the joint together. This will make the assembly of the joint easier.

1 Carefully drive the joint home either by squeezing it in the vice or using a hammer and piece of scrapwood.

2 If everything fits together well, take the joint apart and coat the matching surfaces with glue using a small brush.

3 Reverse the template to the "tails" mode and lock into position with the tightening screws. Then set up the ROUTER with the appropriate dovetail bit and guide bushing (refer to the manufacturer's manual). Mark the thickness of the other piece of wood to indicate the shoulder line of the joint, and set the depth of cut accordingly on the router.

4 Carefully rout the waste away to form the dovetails. A little practice is needed to avoid grain tear as the cutter comes out of the wood. Masking tape can help prevent fibers from splitting.

5 Remove the tails piece and insert the pins piece in the jig, marking the shoulder line as before.

Reverse the jig template and position according to the appropriate guide marks on the jig. Insert the appropriate straight bit in the router and set to depth. First make a series of shallow cuts across the width of the pins.

6 You can see by the profile of the jig fingers how the dovetail bit and the straight bit are used on their respective pieces. Here the straight bit removes the waste for the pins in a series of fine cuts. After a little practice the jig can be fine tuned to such a degree that finished dovetails will squeeze together by hand without any gaps showing. Glue and clamp as for the hand-cut dovetail.

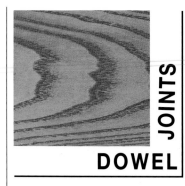

DOWEL JOINTS

The dowel joint is quick and simple to make because it consists of using small wooden pegs instead of hand-cut wood. It offers a versatile and strong system of connecting wood, requiring limited equipment. The joint can form any configuration of pieces, such as "L" shaped, "T" shaped, "X" shaped, etc., and it is often used instead of the mortise-and-tenon. To ensure the joint is strong, several dowels are used instead of the single tenon.

CHECKLIST

Steel ruler and marking gauge
Dowel rods
Appropriate size dowel drilling bit
Drill depth-stop collar
Dowel jig or dowel centers or brads and pliers
White or yellow glue
Clamps
— ⚡ —
Electric power drill
— ✚ —
See pages 8-9

The joint comprises two pieces butted or mitered together (see BUTT AND RABBET JOINTS) with a series of carefully aligned drill holes to accommodate the wood dowel. Normally the dowel is made of a sturdy wood, such as beech or maple, manufactured in short lengths of three main diameters – $\frac{1}{4}$, $\frac{5}{16}$, and $\frac{3}{8}$ inch – with flutings or grooves to allow the glue to disperse evenly. Without these the dowel can act as a piston and compress the glue in the hole. The quickest and most accurate method of dowel jointing is to use commercial dowel center points or a locating/drilling jig, both of which are readily available from good tool stores (see also JOINTS).

MULTI-DOWEL JOINT

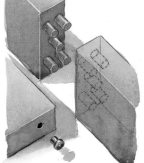

Using several dowels instead of one is the modern equivalent of the mortise-and-tenon joint. Small brass centering points help to secure the joint.

Making a dowel joint with dowel center points

1 After the wood has been accurately prepared to size (see SQUARING WOOD), mark the center lines on the end of the wood using try square, steel ruler and marking gauge.

2 Select the appropriate-diameter dowel center point and with the same diameter drill-bit, drill the holes. You should position yourself in line with the wood so that you can guide the drill parallel to the sides of the wood. To ensure you do not drill in too far, use tape or a readymade depth-stop attached to the drill-bit.

Dowel-locating device

A simple alternative to dowel center points is to use a brad as a dowel-locating device. Drive the pin in and take off the head with a pair of cutters or pliers. Locate the matching hole and after the pieces have been pressed together, withdraw the brad with the cutters or pliers.

Using a doweling jig

1 Mark the positions of the dowel joints by squaring a line across the wood. No matter how good the tool you are using is, the initial marking is critical. The golden rule in all woodwork is, measure twice, and cut once. Clamp the dowel jig to the bench, and clamp the wood with the marked line visible in the center of the jig drilling hole.

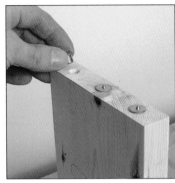

3 It is important to use a special dowel bit which has a center point to locate accurately the marked position. Twist-drills are liable to wander. Flat-bits can sometimes be used, but they have a long center point which is not suitable for drilling into thin boards.

4 For marking the positions on the corresponding piece, insert the dowel center barrels into the holes.

5 Use the pointed end to mark the corresponding drill hole positions. For a "T"-shaped joint, you can square a guide line across the wood, with which the edge of the first piece can align. Then either press or drive the pieces together.

6 Drill out the corresponding holes, taking care to drill straight and square; this can be tricky, so be careful! Apply glue to the dowel rod, the dowel holes, and the edge of the boards, and clamp the work together (see GLUING).

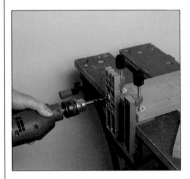

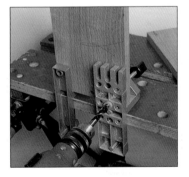

2 Using the appropriate dowel bit and with the depth-stop attached, carefully drill through the guide hole in the jig, straight into the wood. Move the wood along to drill subsequent holes in the same manner.

3 Now insert the other piece of wood into the jig, using the clamps in the adjacent position. Align the marked positions with the jig-drilling hole.

4 Drill out the holes in turn. The jig clamps will need to be re-arranged to drill all the holes.

5 The dowel joint should align perfectly ready for GLUING.

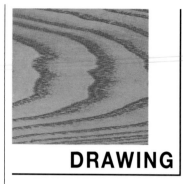

DRAWING

Many woodworkers regard drawing as an unnecessary chore; some even find it daunting. Indeed it is not vital to be able to draw when working with wood other than to possess basic MEASURING AND LAYING OUT skills.

However, if you wish to become a versatile practitioner of this craft, an ability to draw and understand drawings is a great advantage. This is true whether you wish to design your own woodwork or merely copy plans. Only a genius could conceive of and execute a new piece of work without resorting to some kind of drawing or visualization on paper, even if only on the back of an envelope.

CHECKLIST

Drawing board or piece of melamine-faced ¾ inch particle board
or something similar
T-square
30 degree and 45 degree triangle squares
24-inch plastic ruler
Protractor
French curves
Scaled ruler
Pair of compasses
Various grades of pencil
Felt-tips or drawing pens
Masking tape or thumb tacks

Getting ideas on paper

1 With a little practice, quick freehand perspective sketching comes easily. You may prefer to use a felt-tip pen or a soft-leaded pencil, such as a 2B.

2 The hand naturally draws lines in a clean sweep (the wrist serves as a pivot point), so constantly turn the paper to draw each line with ease.

3 A series of light lines can build up the picture quickly. Then go over with a bolder line for the outline. Leading edges are usually thickened. (In most drawing there are three types of line, a feint projection line, the outline, and the dimension line.)

Drawing circles

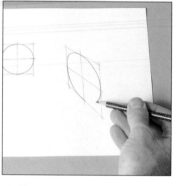

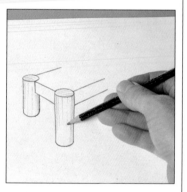

1 Perspective circles or curves can be drawn within a grid, which can be very helpful! Try drawing the circle first within a quartered box, then draw the same box at an angle and fill in the curves. Remember to rotate the paper and use your hand naturally.

After a while you will be able to draw perspective circles freehand. Remember that it is an ellipse which has its long arc perpendicular to the walls of the cylindrical object to be drawn.

2 Circular solids can be shaded to give depth. Imagine a series of equidistant points marked around the circle with lines extended vertically.

Translating sketches into working drawings

1 More accurate drawings can be achieved on a drawing board with T-square, triangle square, and ruler. First set up the paper on the board using masking tape. You need H and 2H pencils. When working with a T-square, always make sure it is tight against the edge of the board.

2 Plans for woodworking usually consist of a front elevation, end elevation, and a plan (bird's-eye view). There are two conventions, first-angle and third-angle projections. A horizontal and vertical axis are drawn first with a hard-leaded pencil.

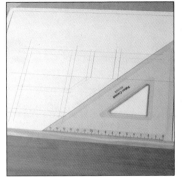

3 Shared information such as the height of the object to be drawn, its width, and other features can be extended or projected in feint lines to all three elevations. Transferring this information from the plan to the end elevation can be achieved with the 45-degree triangle square.

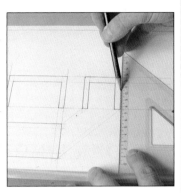

4 The outline then depicts each elevation boldly and, as a general rule, the projection line should not be seen beyond arm's length (provided you have used a 2H pencil). Hidden details can be shown on each elevation using a dotted-line convention.

5 Dimension lines are then included in the drawing, spreading the information evenly across the three elevations.

You will probably need to make working drawings to scale, say one-fifth scale. Specially scaled rulers can be used for this purpose.

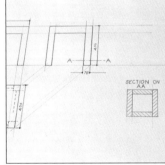

6 To be useful, a working drawing requires the addition of detailed information which needs further clarification. Enlarged detailed elevations or sections can be drawn elsewhere on the paper, cross-referring with a code such as "Section AA."

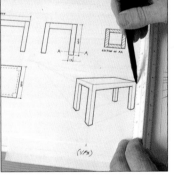

7 You may wish to trace the entire working drawing using a felt-tip or drawing pen on tracing paper to implement a perspective view of the object which has been separately drawn. This helps balance the layout of the drawing. Either tape the sheets down or use heavy (but clean) objects to anchor the paper while drawing.

8 A useful application of simple technical drawing in woodworking is the construction of a cutting list.

DRILLING

The technique of drilling accurately is one of the first things to learn in the workshop. Modern methods have made this considerably easier.

Holes are "drilled" by the removal of wood fibers with an "Archimedes-screw"-type bit which is rotated at speed in the chuck of a hand or power drill. The fibers are severed and cleared from the hole by the drill flutings or grooves.

Holes can also be cut by the scraping action of a spade or flat-bit which is specifically designed for a power drill. Hand-drilling has been largely superseded by the more efficient power drill which can be hand-held or fixed in a drill stand.

Power drilling

The portable electric drill gave birth to the power-tool revolution. Early power-tool attachments for the drill included jigsaws, circular saws (see SAWING), and sanders (see ABRADING). There is hardly a workshop without a portable drill. These adaptable machines can be easily mounted into a vertical drill stand for precise and accurate drilling on the bench.

Most drills are cord-operated, with keyed chucks for gripping the bit firmly. They are rated by wattage (average 500 watts) and chuck capacity, (⅜-½ inch), which refers to the maximum size of bit which can be fitted. The advantage of modern flat-bits is that wide holes, up to 1½ inches, can be achieved from a ¼ inch shank diameter.

Less torque (twisting power) is required to operate flat-bits, but purists argue that they tear wood fibers rather than cutting them cleanly, and the twist-drill is preferred for general accuracy. However, twist-drills are liable to wander in the wood, especially in end grain, and it is preferable to use a wood-bit which has a defined center point.

Drilling pilot holes

For drilling small pilot holes (see HINGES AND LOCKS), a tiny twist-bit is used, as flat-bits are seldom available in diameters less than ¼ inch. You can of course profile or shape your own flat-bits using a bench grinder (see TOOL MAINTENANCE).

Cordless or battery-operated portable drills are popular, although they are less powerful than cord-operated drills. They offer convenience in and out of the workshop. Being low voltage (3.6-24 volts), cordless power tools are safer electrically.

Recharging of batteries can be achieved in as little as five minutes, and it always pays to carry spares. These drills are handy for working a long way from a power supply and, from a safety point of view, for working in wet conditions.

The keyed chuck has been replaced to a large extent by the keyless chuck, which offers adequate grip for the drill-bit. Such drills with their torque-adjusted clutches can double as powered screwdrivers.

There are numerous attachments which will fit into power drills, ranging from hinge-sinking cutters to rotary rasps and abrading disks.

CHECKLIST

Power drill (hammer action not vital)
Power drill stand
Set of twist-bits
Set of flat-bits
Countersink bit

+

See pages 8-9

SELECTION OF TWIST-DRILLS AND SPADE BITS

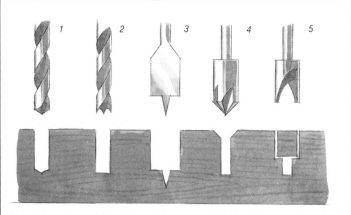

1 Twist-bit for making small holes; also useful for waste clearance and starting screws. 2 Doweling bit for setting wooden dowels needing a square-bottomed hole. 3 Spade bit works with a scraping action, cuts large holes very rapidly. 4 The countersink bit is to allow a wood screw head to lie flush with the work's surface. 5 The plug cutter removes waste in one piece to allow it to be replaced later.

How to use a hand-held power drill

1 Insert the required drill-bit into the chuck, making sure it is tightened with the key in all three holes.

2 When marking positions for drilling holes, a cross is generally used to denote the center. For end grain drilling, it is preferable to use a drill-bit which has a clearly defined center point.

3 Clasp your hands around the drill comfortably, positioning yourself above the work, locate the drill-bit, and begin drilling.
  Occasionally withdraw the drill-bit in order to clear the chips, which have a tendency to clog and overheat.

4 When drilling straight through holes, it is important to stop drilling when the point of the flat-bit appears through the wood, then turn the work around and drill from the other side; this is to prevent splitting or what is known as "breakout."

Using a drill stand

1 Install the drill in the drill stand, making sure it is secure, and insert the correct bit, using the chuck key to secure it.

2 Place scrapwood underneath the work for straight-through holes. For blind holes (holes which do not go all the way through), you will need to set the depth-stop on the drill stand.
  Carefully hold down the work with one hand, anticipating the rotary snatching of the drill-bit (especially wide-diameter flat-bits). Switch on the power with your other hand and gently lower the bit into the wood.

3 Countersunk holes (for sinking the screw head level with the surface of the wood, or deeper) can be achieved by setting the depth-stop.

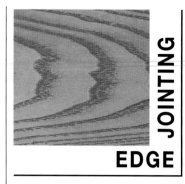

EDGE JOINTING

When wide boards or panels are required, you will find it is usually necessary to join together narrower pieces along their edges to make up the width. Boards vary in width, according to the species of tree from which they are cut. It is very rare for a table top, for instance, to be made from a single board, even from a wide-girth tree such as mahogany.

Of course the problem does not exist when using manufactured boards such as plywood, MDF, or particle board, because they are available in much larger sizes, such as 4 × 8 feet, and by their composition they also avoid the problem of warping or otherwise twisting out of shape.

If you look at the end grain of any solid board, you will notice the annual rings (more pronounced on some woods than others). A rule of thumb is that the annual rings will try to straighten out when the wood dries. This gives you an indication of which way the board will warp. If the annual rings are long, it means the board has been "plane sawn" from the tree and is likely to warp more than a board with short annual rings (which is "quarter" or "radial" sawn).

There are various methods of edge-jointing. The simplest method is to joint the boards edge to edge and glue and clamp them (see GLUING). For a stronger and more long-lasting bond, the edge joint can be reinforced with DOWELS, BISCUITS, or by using a long loose plywood tongue which slots into both faces of the joint. By using a special bit in a router, you can also make a "tongue-and-groove" joint or a milled joint. These methods not only improve the mechanical strength, but also lengthen the glue line across the section of the wood.

CHECKLIST

Steel ruler and try square
¼-inch straight bit
¼-inch birch plywood
2–4 bar clamps
White or yellow glue
or
Plastic resin glue
Water bowl and cloth

———

Handplane

———

Planer-thicknesser
Biscuit jointer or
power drill, dowel jig and dowels
or router

———

See pages 8-9

HOW TO PREVENT WARPING WHEN EDGE-JOINTING

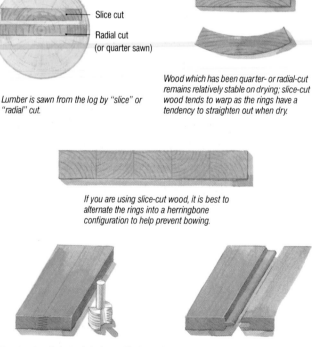

Slice cut

Radial cut
(or quarter sawn)

Lumber is sawn from the log by "slice" or "radial" cut.

Wood which has been quarter- or radial-cut remains relatively stable on drying; slice-cut wood tends to warp as the rings have a tendency to straighten out when dry.

If you are using slice-cut wood, it is best to alternate the rings into a herringbone configuration to help prevent bowing.

For extra strength, instead of using a rubbed joint (as in the herringbone arrangement above), a milled joint can be made using a special router bit.

Large areas can be paneled with tongue-and-groove board, as shrinkage is taken up in the joint.

Edge-jointing a small panel

1 Square some 4- × ¾-inch boards (see SQUARING WOOD). Select the boards for visual interest (varying the grain and color) and arrange them in a "herringbone" fashion to minimize wood movement. Number the boards, as you will need this for future reference when assembling them.

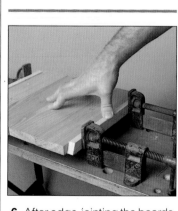

6 After edge-jointing the boards, clamp them together to check that everything pulls up accurately. This is called "dry clamping" (see GLUING).

2 Check that the edges of the boards are perfectly "square" and straight. If you have planed the wood by machine, it is easier to achieve accuracy. It is important that the boards fit well, and you should not rely on excessive clamping pressure to pull them in. Take your time and it is not too difficult to get right.

3 Check that the board edges are perfectly flat with a steel ruler or straightedge.

4 You can edge-joint the boards by a variety of methods ranging from a simple EDGE-TO-EDGE JOINT, DOWEL JOINT, BISCUIT JOINT, or loose tongues.

5 Biscuit jointing is a quick and effective method for edge-jointing and relies on a series of marks on the edge for the center of the biscuit.

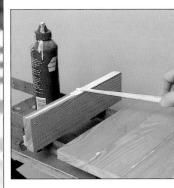

7 Apply glue to the joint surfaces and the inserts, and place the whole assembly in clamps. For longer panels you will need to use perhaps three or four bar clamps, placing some on top to prevent bowing.

8 After checking that all the boards are flush (flat and level), persuading them with hammer and scrapwood if necessary, wipe away the excess glue with a damp cloth. This is very important and saves unnecessary work afterward.

9 Leave the boards in the clamps (at least 2 hours for white or yellow and 8 hours for plastic resin glue), then remove the panel and clean up the surfaces with a finely adjusted handplane. Working diagonally gives the most efficient cut (see PLANING).

10 Alternatively you can use a finely set powered handplaner and gently skim over the surface.

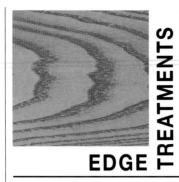

EDGE TREATMENTS

In much period furniture, the edges of wood panels (for example, carcasses, shelves, table tops) were seldom left plain or "square," but were profiled in some way to add visual interest. These sometimes ornate profiles are called moldings, and they serve also to soften the edges for more comfortable handling. Moldings are also often put on to other wood artifacts solely for esthetic reasons, as in the case of picture or window frames.

Today there is a practical need for treating the edges of furniture for both tactile and visual reasons, especially as much of it is made of veneered particle board. The brittle edges of this cheap substitute for solid wood need reinforcing with solid wood strips called "edge banding." This can be done before the panel is VENEERED, so that the edges blend in discreetly with the face veneer, using the same material for the edge banding. Edge banding is usually at least ¼ inch wide, offering depth for molded profiles similar to those used in solid wood construction.

Traditional moldings used to be cut with differently profiled handplanes, and there is an interesting vocabulary of profiles such as carvetto, ogee, cove, reed, and astragal. Many of these planes are now collectors' items, and woodworkers of all ages are keen to acquire them for largely sentimental reasons.

Present day routing technology has, to a large extent, replaced the old molding planes and a vast range of profiled router bits for shaping edges is used instead (see ROUTING).

CHECKLIST

Measuring tools
Sandpaper
Glue
Masking tape or clamps
——————
Smoothing or jack plane
——————
Router and bits
——————
See pages 8-9

Types of edges

1 The simplest edge is a "square" edge, which can be achieved with a handplane or by machine PLANING.

A SELECTION OF APPLIED AND CUT MOLDINGS

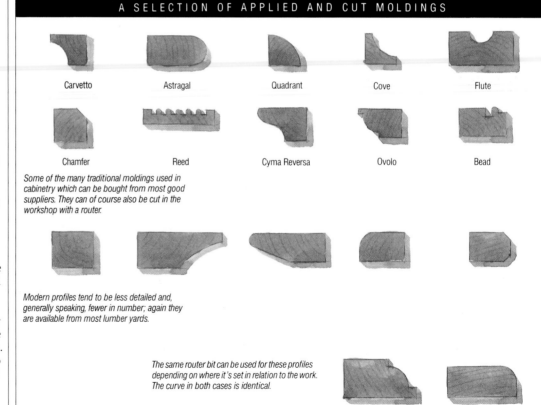

Carvetto Astragal Quadrant Cove Flute

Chamfer Reed Cyma Reversa Ovolo Bead

Some of the many traditional moldings used in cabinetry which can be bought from most good suppliers. They can of course also be cut in the workshop with a router.

Modern profiles tend to be less detailed and, generally speaking, fewer in number; again they are available from most lumber yards.

The same router bit can be used for these profiles depending on where it's set in relation to the work. The curve in both cases is identical.

2 If you want to make a thicker board look thinner or more delicate, plane a chamfer (or slope) along the bottom edge, first using a marking gauge and then planing to the line.

3 All edges of furniture should be slightly softened with very fine sandpaper. This removes the sharp edge which is known as an "arris" making the edge soft on both the eye and the hand.

Using a router to make molded edges

1 A variety of molded edges can be achieved by using the ROUTER and fence, set up with a profiled bit. It is sometimes hard to visualize a profile because it is the exact opposite of the shape of the router bit. When in doubt, simply make a final cut on a piece of waste wood and if you like the shape, use it.

2 Some router bits have ball-bearing guides and can therefore follow concave and convex edges. Afterwards you need to finish the molded section with sandpaper.

Applying edge banding to a veneered panel

1 Make sure the edges of the manufactured board are true and square. This is very simply done with a try square, but make sure that the stock of the square rests firmly against the surface of the board.

2 Prepare to size some ¼-inch wide edge banding, which should be fractionally thicker than the particle board. MITER the corners and then glue and tape the edge banding in position on the edges.

3 With a handplane, trim the edge banding flush ready for VENEERING. Work inward to avoid splitting the grain. After the panel has been veneered, the edges can be profiled as though they are solid wood, provided the edge banding is wide enough.

FINISHING

Most objects in wood usually require a protective coating of some kind, depending on their function and environment. This coating is invariably known as a "finish." It greatly enhances the visual appeal of a piece of furniture, and different woods demand different finishes such as lacquers, oils, waxes, or stains.

In some cases it is better to leave the wood in its bare natural state. Some Danish furniture in the past has been left bare and by subsequent scrubbing with soap solution a natural luster has evolved.

Arguably a highly lacquered finish acts as a barrier to the natural material, and this can be a drawback, especially as wood is a warm tactile material.
But generally it is an advantage to apply some kind of lacquer or oil to give a protective coating to the wood.

Some woodworkers believe that the wood should always "breathe" and that a fine oil or microporous lacquer should be applied; others would prefer to totally seal the wood which helps inhibit wood movement, due to the loss or intake of moisture in the air. Conventional lacquers can be up to 40 percent impermeable whereas epoxy resin coatings are up to 100 percent impermeable and can withstand excessive heat. Finishing is both science and art, and is often a hot topic of debate among woodworkers. You should never be afraid to experiment with finishes, and you will probably establish preferences, not least because of the smell which some finishes have.

Prior to finishing, the project should be filled, if there are knots, holes, or blemishes, then sanded smooth by hand or power sander (see ABRADING). All marks should be removed with edges slightly softened, or rounded, with the sandpaper.

CHECKLIST

Wood filler, fine sandpaper, and block
Polishing pad and cotton
Variety of soft brushes
Nitrocellulose lacquer
Lacquer thinner (acetone)
Wax polish
Very fine steel wool
Soft burnishing cloth
Polyurethane varnish
Mineral spirits or turpentine
Danish oil
Linseed oil
Turpentine or mineral spirits
Water stain or alcohol stain
Two-part epoxy resin

See pages 8-9

Preparing the surface

1 Whatever finish you are using, surfaces need to be carefully prepared. In this sequence a wood filler is made from sanded dust taken from the item to be lacquered, mixed with a drop of nitrocellulose lacquer. In this way you can always be sure that the color is right. A fine putty knife helps to work the filler into any knot holes.

2 After filling any unsightly holes, lightly sand the surface with 400 grit sandpaper and a block.

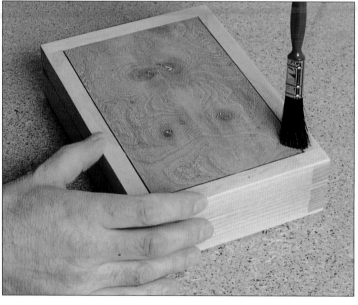

3 Remove any residual dust by blowing or by using a brush. In this case the dust has to be removed from a fine groove in the lid of the jewelry box.

Applying nitrocellulose lacquer with a pad

Nitrocellulose lacquer is a fast-drying convenient finish, available in gloss, satin, or flat. It can be applied with a brush or pad. A good idea is to use a lacquer jar and to make a plywood brush holder which also acts as the lid to prevent the lacquer from hardening, especially on the brush.

Because of the speed at which the lacquer cures (in seconds), you will find a pad easier to control and gives better results. The pad is made of wads of cotton wrapped in a piece of cotton or linen.

Nitrocellulose lacquer is tougher than french polish, but softer than polyurethane varnish. It is often sprayed (after thinning). Equipment/brushes are cleaned with acetone, which is a readily available solvent.

1 Having prepared the surface, load the pad with lacquer and partially drain away the excess against the lip of the container.

2 Work the pad swiftly in circular motions across the surface. Note how the beauty of the grain is enhanced and how the wood takes on a rich luster.

3 Then work the pad lightly along the grain and parallel to the edge. The knack is to apply a little lacquer quickly and build up 2 or 3 coats with a few minutes' interval.

4 The entire box can be finished in one operation. If you apply the lacquer very thinly, it will be touch-dry in seconds. After 2 coats of lacquer have been applied – with 20 minutes between coats and an hour to harden finally – the lacquer can be de-nibbed (lightly rubbed down to remove any small rough spots) with 400 grit sandpaper or wax polished with fine steel wool.

Applying a wax polish

You can apply waxes directly to bare wood, but ideally the grain should be sealed by lacquering first. Not all woods should be waxed – open-grained woods can attract the dirt and are best left varnished.

After preparing the surface, dip a small wad of fine steel wool into the wax polish and lightly rub it into the grain, finishing with the grain direction. Finish with a soft dry cloth to polish the surface to a luster.

French polishing with a pad

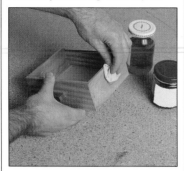

French polish (also known as white polish and button polish) is a quick-drying "traditional" finish which is thinned with denatured alcohol. It is softer than nitrocellulose lacquer and is applied in several coats with half an hour or so between them.

Prepare the surface, then apply the french polish with a pad, similar to the application of nitrocellulose lacquer. Apply a little polish using a fast circular motion.

Applying a polyurethane varnish with a brush

This is a durable general-purpose varnish available in gloss, satin, or flat finish, suitable for interior and exterior woodwork.

Generally 2 to 3 coats are desirable. To obtain a deeper penetration, thin the first coat by up to 20 percent using mineral spirit. Polyurethanes take about 2 hours to dry (6 hours between coats) and allow you a few minutes "working time."

1 First you should "break in" a new brush by roughing it against a clean stone surface. This will make it flexible and also get rid of any loose hairs which might otherwise spoil the finish. Dip the brush into the varnish and wipe off half of it against the edge of the varnish can.

2 Now brush the varnish quickly and evenly across the project. You do not have to go with the grain initially.

Applying an oil finish

Suitable oils, such as linseed, danish oil (or teak oil), are applied by brush or cloth. Oils are generally most suitable for exterior woodwork as they are water repellent, and they give an excellent luster to certain woods. As oils are absorbed deep into the fibers, it helps to thin the first coat by up to 20 percent (using mineral spirits).

Applying a wood stain

1 Wood stains are generally oil- or water-based, the former being easier to apply and the latter deeper penetrating. Alternatives can be used effectively. Subtle color-fast applications of artists' oil paint, for instance, can be used, followed by a turpentine-based lacquer.

Prepare the surface. Apply a water stain with a pad or brush. Subsequent wiping off with a damp cloth can improve the consistency of the finish.

2 A black stain is used to fill the open pores in this piece of ash. It is then rapidly wiped off, allowing the grain and figure of the wood to show through. This gives an aging effect to the wood which many people find pleasing. It's a good idea to experiment on a piece of scrapwood of the same type first.

Applying a varnish stain

Applying epoxy resins

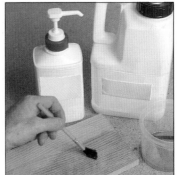

3 After the entire surface has been saturated with varnish, brush lightly at a shallow angle parallel to the edges to avoid drips and runs.

4 Tilt the project up (you will have to varnish the underside after the first side has dried) and work the brush lightly and swiftly along the grain, checking against the reflection of light for runs.

Varnish stains can be applied by brush in exactly the same way as clear varnishes. A first coat of clear varnish can be applied or the varnish stain applied straight onto bare wood.

When applying a varnish stain to either sealed or bare wood, the final brush strokes should go along the grain. Two coats may be necessary.

Epoxy resins which cure (or harden) by heat with a chemical catalyst are extremely hard, durable, and water and chemical resistant. They come in two separate containers and need to be mixed shortly before use. They are commonly known as "two-part" adhesives. They can also withstand very high temperatures and are almost totally impervious.

After mixing the epoxy with its catalyst in a mixing container, apply it thickly with a brush. You should take care to avoid runs on vertical edges. The epoxy must be left to cure for at least a day and then rubbed down between coats. To achieve an immaculate finish, you will find it is necessary to apply several coats, rigorously rubbed down with fine sandpaper between.

SPRAY FINISHING

Spraying is a quick and efficient method of applying finishes.

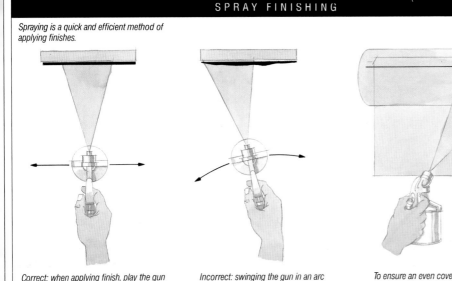

Correct: when applying finish, play the gun in smooth, steady sweeps, keeping the spray parallel to the surface.

Incorrect: swinging the gun in an arc produces patchy coverage and causes runs.

To ensure an even coverage, overlap each stroke by 50 percent, and spray past the ends of the pieces.

FRETWORK

There is probably no better introduction to the world of woodworking than fretwork, especially for youngsters, for it is a creative, enjoyable, and basically safe pastime. Fretwork is a gentle and delicate technique in which wood as thin as $1/16$ inch can be intricately cut, usually to a prescribed pattern, template, or line, for decorative or functional applications. It is probably true to say that 90 percent of applications are decorative, although many toys and jigsaw puzzles are also made by this technique. The fretsaw also has applications in engineering patternmaking, where it is often used to cut non-ferrous metals.

Nowadays the electric scroll saw has superseded the hand fretsaw, and its quiet reciprocating action makes it one of the safest machines to use.

Compared with most other woodworking saws, the scroll saw blade is fine-toothed (there are numerous tooth options) and is easy to install in the machine. The scroll saw can cut all manner of curves, some extremely tight, in woods up to $3/4$ inch or $1\frac{1}{8}$ inch, and some machines have tilting tables allowing angled cuts up to 45 degrees to be made. The scroll saw is generally specified by its throat capacity. This is the distance between the blade and the back of the machine measured across the flat of the cutting blade. A machine with a 16-inch throat could, for example, cut across a board 32 inches wide, if the operator reversed the board end-for-end during the cutting process.

CHECKLIST

Assortment of thin materials (plywood, etc.)

Powered scroll saw
Selection of blades

See pages 8-9

Powered fretwork using thin wood

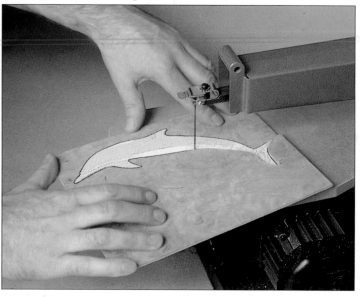

Draw, trace, or paste the desired shape onto a piece of thin plywood, such as $1/8$-inch veneered plywood. It is easier at first to use thin wood with a fine-toothed blade which can cut tight corners. Sometimes if the corner is too tight, it's a good idea to back the blade out of the cut and to start another cut from a different angle. Look at the ventral (bottom) fin of a shark, and you can see how difficult it would be to turn in such a tight spot. If you started another cut in line with the top edge of the fin, you could come right up to the body and cut away the waste quite easily.

Insert the blade with its teeth pointing downward. The wood will want to snatch up, so hold it down firmly while you are cutting. Keep your fingers clear of the blade and blow away the dust as you cut. Many scroll saws nowadays are fitted with blowers which clear away the sawdust while you are working. These normally consist of a small plastic tube near the blade which is connected to bellows operated by the up-and-down movement of the saw arm.

Powered fretwork using thick wood

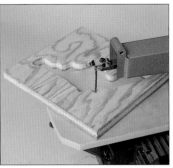

1 To fret thick wood, such as ¾-inch plywood, use a medium-toothed blade. This is because it has a more robust cutting job to do and is thus less likely to break in thicker wood. Holding the wood firmly down, slowly feed the wood into the blade. You can sense the speed of cut by the sound and feel. Never try to force the rate of feed into the blade. At best the blade will overheat, and at worst it will break.

2 Cut tight curves slowly; again this is to prevent overheating and blade breakage. The finish left from the scroll saw blade is remarkably smooth, which is a great advantage in toymaking where delicate little fingers will become involved with the finished article.

JOHN ANDERSON
Box
This intriguing box, which is made of jelutong (lime), was bandsawn. The outline of the box was drawn onto the wood and a slice removed. The box section itself, the "hull" of the boat, was cut out with a fretsaw. The outline slice was then glued back on the original block and the profile cut out. The process was repeated to form the drawer section. The box was finished in acrylic paints, a shellac seal, and a wax finish.

Working enclosed cuts

When making an enclosed cut, for example one which does not come to the edge of the wood, there is obviously a problem in getting the blade initially to pass through the wood. This is done by first drilling a hole in the part of the wood which is to be removed; disconnecting the blade at one end in the saw; threading the blade through the hole, and re-connecting it. As always, you should shade in the part to be cut out to avoid mistakes. It is remarkably easy to cut away the wrong bit, especially when working on complicated patterns.

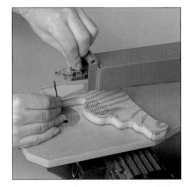

1 For enclosed cuts remove the blade from the scroll saw by slackening the tension adjuster. Then feed the blade through the hole you have drilled in the wood and re-attach it to the scroll saw ready for cutting.

2 Hold the wood down securely and carefully cut to the line. Check your fingers are always away from the blade.

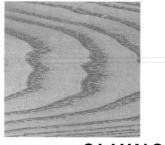

GLUING

Most items of woodwork rely on glue to hold them together. Very few wood joints or wood components stay together solely by mechanical means, unless they are specifically designed to do so (as in the case of "knockdown furniture" or some very intricate Japanese JOINTS). The mortise-and-tenon, for example, was originally a dry joint and was held together by adding pins. Until quite recently, glues were liable to degrade over a period of time, causing furniture to fall apart; today the notion of a "permanent" bond is as familiar in woodworking as it is in metalworking, where epoxy glues are often used instead of welds. Modern woodworking glues are stronger than the surrounding wood fibers, and when something breaks it is unlikely to be along the glue line.

Gluing can vary in complexity from the relatively simple gluing of a "rubbed" joint (two pieces glued edge to edge and slid against each other to form a suction) to the gluing and clamping of numerous parts of a carcass.

Gluing usually requires constant pressure throughout the curing period, and hence gluing and clamping is an integral process and a vital stage in the making of a piece of woodwork.

Careful preparation is required to avoid disastrous results, and usually "dry clamping" is executed to check that clamps and other equipment are immediately on hand and set to position.

CHECKLIST

White or yellow glue
Plastic resin glue
Water
Spatula or brush
Cloth
"C" clamps and bar clamps
Epoxy resin glue
Denatured alcohol or acetone

+

See pages 8-9

Gluing a "rubbed" joint

1 The essence of this simple joint for thin boards is in the accurate planing of the two contact surfaces (SEE PLANING and SQUARING WOOD). After this has been checked, apply white or yellow glue to one surface and spread it out evenly.

2 Against a flat surface (such as the bench protected with paper), use a sliding motion to rub both pieces vigorously. This squeezes out the glue and creates a suction. There is no need for clamps. Leave the panel to dry for 2 hours in a warm environment.

Gluing and clamping frameworks using bar clamps

1 Use scrapwood blocks with the clamps to prevent bruising or marking. To maintain squareness, align the center of the clamp with the center of the thickness of the wood.

2 Check with a try square and move the clamps fractionally to adjust squareness if this should be necessary.

Gluing a stack laminated panel

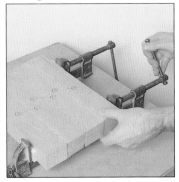   

1 After accurately preparing the separate pieces of wood to size, mount them in two bar clamps to check their alignment. This is called "dry clamping" and is essential for most glue-and-clamp operations. You can number the pieces with location marks to ensure perfect alignment.

2 Arrange the glue contact edges uppermost and apply white or yellow glue swiftly with a brush to each piece in turn. Locate each piece to the coded marks. If the work is large, use a longer-drying plastic resin glue; white or yellow glue only allows 2 or 3 minutes' working time.

3 Use a hammer and scrapwood to align the pieces before the final clamping pressure is applied.

4 It is likely the wood will "wander" a little under pressure, in which case slacken off the clamps and re-align the wood. When the pieces are finally clamped, wipe off excessive glue with a damp cloth.

3 For checking to see if frames (and carcasses) are square, a diagonal rod can be used to check the opposing internal dimensions. These must of course be exactly the same.

Gluing a small carcass

The carcass consists of four sides with a top and base – a lot of clamping! It can be clamped in stages (for example, the body first) or achieved all at once, using masking tape for initial alignment of the pieces. Virtually all available space has been taken up by a "C" clamp. This happens often in clamping, which only emphasizes the need for good preparation as all gluing is done "against the clock."

Epoxy "fillet" bonding

1 Epoxy resins are two-part adhesives (resin and hardener) and should be mixed to the manufacturers' specification. Epoxies are extremely strong; their added strength allows "piece" or "spline" bonding, whereby thin material can be reinforced by the epoxy running into the corner.

After applying the resin, tilt the structure so that the resin flows along the joint.

2 To make the adhesive easier to apply, microfiber filler or colloidal silica can be mixed into the resin (after the hardener has been mixed). A slightly thicker mix prevents overabsorption of the glue around the joint area. Thicker mixes can be used when joint accuracy is not crucial and the resin acts as a filler-glue, or when using a brush, to "feather" the piece on right-angle thin-material bends.

Gluing a dovetail joint

1 A dovetail joint has an extended gluing contact area, and it is best to use a glue – such as urea-formaldehyde – with a longer pot life. First check the joint fits "dry."

2 Mix up the glue with the powder, then add small amounts of water – never the other way around. Allow 4 parts glue to 1 part water.

3 To avoid lumps mix a thick paste and thin it with water gradually.

4 When the glue runs off like molasses, it is correctly mixed. Leave it to stand for a few minutes. The pot life of urea-formaldehyde is about 10 to 20 minutes, after which it thickens and becomes unusable.

5 Using a brush, thinly apply the glue to both surfaces.

6 Tap the joint together using a hammer and scrapwood along the shoulder line.

7 Then place the scrapwood between the joint "fingers" and gently hammer down to make good shoulder-line contact.

8 A cutaway clamping block should be used to allow for the slight joint protrusion. Check for squareness with a try square, and leave the whole assembly to cure for at least 8 hours.

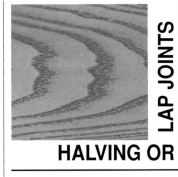

LAP JOINTS

HALVING OR

Strong, attractive, and quick to make, the halving or lap joint has many applications. It is one of woodworking's strongest wood joints because equal portions are removed from each member and optimum fiber overlap ensures the strongest leverage in one direction. Therefore one member is not weakened any more than the other because in all halving or lap joints, both members are always the same thickness. Where they overlap, that portion which is removed from one member is replaced by the wood left on the other. However, until fairly recently, the joint relied on nails or screws as well as glue to hold it together. The advent of modern "permanent" glues has now made it a truly versatile joint for "L," "T," and "X" configurations in frames and some modern "permanent" glues are quite sufficient to hold it in both indoor and outdoor applications, without any further assistance.

The basic technique for cutting all the configurations of this joint are the same, but it's useful here to look at the "X" configuration because, of the three, it is both the strongest and most commonly used.

Cutting an "X" halving or lap joint by hand

1 After preparing the wood to size (see SQUARING WOOD), trace the width of each piece on the corresponding piece with a pencil or ballpoint pen.

2 Using a try square held with the stock against the face side of the wood, extend the marks both across the wood and to halfway down the edges.

3 With a marking gauge set to exactly half the thickness of the wood, gauge the depth lines using the stock of the gauge against the face side. Shade in the waste (see MEASURING AND LAYING OUT).

CHECKLIST

Pencil or ballpoint pen
Marking gauge
——☛——
Try square
Tenon saw
Chisel
Mallet
Hammer and scrapwood
——⚡——
Radial-arm saw
"C" clamp and batten
——✚——
See pages 8-9

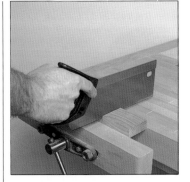

4 Clamp the wood firmly in the vice and saw carefully on the waste side of the line with a tenon saw, to the halfway mark (see SAWING).

5 After sawing the other line, checking it carefully against the width of the other piece, chisel away the waste wood (see CHISELING). Work into the center then turn the wood around and repeat the action to avoid splitting the end fibers. A mallet greatly helps to control the chiseling action.

6 The chiseling is done in approximately ⅛-inch cuts at a time. Make finer chisel cuts as you approach the line.

7 Now check for flatness with the edge of the chisel. Repeat the process on the other piece of wood, checking the position of the sawn lines, which are crucial for a tight fit.

An alternative chisel method is to make tapered cuts from each direction to form a "hilltop," then chisel horizontally back to the line.

8 Carefully chisel a slight "leading edge" where the joint will fit together. This will prevent too much pressure having to be applied and will gradually ease the two halves into position.

9 Squeeze the joint together by using a vice. If it is too tight, plane a fraction off the side edges in preference to chiseling back the saw line; chiseling is difficult to do accurately because the error is likely to be very fine, and you would be chiseling across the grain in small bites. Then clean up the surfaces using a smoothing plane.

Cutting an "L" halving or lap joint on the radial-arm saw

This example is for the "L" configuration of the halving or lap joint, but it could be used for any other. The radial-arm saw is predominantly for use in cutting across the grain, where, by taking a series of very closely spaced cuts across the grain of the joint, it eliminates the need to chisel down the grain for cleaning away the waste.

Tightly spaced cuts allow the remaining waste simply to be snapped off. In fact, if the cuts made are close enough together, all the waste will be removed by the saw, and no cleaning up with a chisel will be necessary. Remember that with a saw of this type there will be considerable "set" on the blade, and this will result in a much wider "kerf" or width-of-cut than you will get with a handsaw.

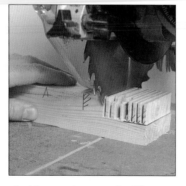

1 After you have marked the wood for width and depth of cut and adjusted the blade height (checking the cut is centered), pull the saw head across in a series of narrow cuts.

2 The narrow strips of "short grain" are easily removed by knocking the wood against a benchtop, and then the surface is perfectly leveled using the radial-arm saw.

3 It should be possible to achieve a perfectly flush joint even if the contact surfaces have to be reworked fractionally on the radial-arm saw.

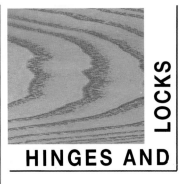

HINGES AND LOCKS

Some advanced woodworkers devise ingenious ways of opening cabinet doors or locking the lids on trinket boxes, etc., without resorting to metal hinges, locks, or catches. A poor quality mass-produced hinge, or crudely designed handle, will certainly let down an otherwise finely crafted cabinet.

Most woodworkers however,

CHECKLIST

Pair of small brass butt hinges with appropriate countersunk (CSK) screws
Marking gauge
Marking knife
Combination square
Bar clamps and wood blocks

———◄———

Small screwdriver
Drill-bits
Chisel
Mallet
Tenon or dovetail saw
Coping saw

———⚡———

Power drill and shank and pilot bit
Router and small straight bit

———✛———

See pages 8-9

whether beginners or highly skilled, will resort to standardized hardware, of which there is now considerable choice for most applications. Choose hardware to suit the job. For example, if you are building a closet door, a pressed steel or brass-plated hinge which is simply screwed onto the surface might be OK, but if you are making a delicate trinket box, a precision-made cast-brass hinge would be called for.

Visual appeal, strength, durability, size, and specific function are important factors to consider when choosing the right hinge, lock, or catch.

Once the choice has been made, you should then select the best tools and woodworking techniques to attach the hardware accurately. As you develop your woodworking skills, you will find that being able to hang a door correctly or to fit a lock which engages properly is both satisfying and extremely useful.

Recessing a brass hinge into a small jewelry box

1 Mount the jewelry box firmly on the bench. A bar clamp held in the vice with an appropriate wood block is convenient. The block between the clamp head and the box is to prevent bruising or marking when the clamp is tightened. The hinge lengths are first marked on the wood with a sharp marking knife. Their positions can be guessed; each one should be nearer the end of the jewelry box than the middle, but do make sure they are both the same.

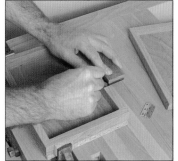

2 Using a try square, lightly square the lines across the wood to the approximate hinge width and down the edge to the approximate hinge thickness.

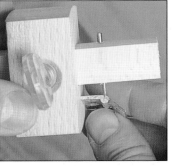

3 Set a marking gauge to width using the hinge itself. Note that the spur (or point of the gauge) is set to the center of the pivot of the hinge. This action is repeated for gauging the depth of the hinge recess. This is very important and ensures the lid and box faces meet exactly.

4 Gauge the width of the hinge recess using the locating points that you marked originally, to prevent overrun of the gauge. Reset the gauge to mark the depth of the hinge recess and repeat the process. Now deepen the squared cut lines to where the marking gauge lines intersect, and shade in the waste.

5 Now mark the opposing hinge lengths on the lid by carefully extending the lines so that the hinges will align perfectly. Then repeat the marking operations.

6 With a mallet and chisel, carefully sever the waste fibers across the grain by a series of fine parallel cuts, say, ½ inch apart. Work from the center moving outward in each direction, carefully locating the chisel for each cut.

7 Now work the chisel horizontally to lift out the severed fibers. After the fibers have been severed across the grain (see CHISELING), carefully pare the fibers back to the line along the grain.

8 The final step is to trim the ends of the recess across the grain to the line.

Using a router to cut a hinge recess

1 An alternative method to cutting a hinge recess is to use a router and a straight bit (see ROUTING). The same marking techniques can still be applied, or the hinge can be held against the router bit to establish the depth of the recess. Making a trial cut in a piece of waste wood is another way of establishing the depth for the recess. One drawback with using a router is that the recess will always finish with curved ends. Finish with a chisel.

2 When using a router, the curve left from the bit has to be removed with the chisel. The final step is to trim the ends of the recess across the grain to the line.

Using a router to cut a lock recess

1 A router set with a straight bit can be used to cut the fine recesses, using again the same techniques as for the hinges.

2 To remove the bulk of the lock recess, plunge the router in a series of overlapping cuts, setting it to a depth-stop. Final trimming of the curved ends is done with the chisel in the same way as cutting hinge recesses.

Inserting hinges

1 Insert a hinge and mark the center hole with a pencil. Then drill a pilot hole fractionally nearer the shoulder (where the long edge of the hinge will butt against) to ensure a tight fit when screwed in.

2 After cutting all four hinge recesses, run a finely set plane along the edge to produce a slight bevel. This allows the lid to swing freely.

3 Now screw the hinges in position, using the correct-width screwdriver to avoid scratching them. In tough woods use a steel screw as a "primer." This means a steel screw is inserted first to widen the pilot hole. Brass screws are much softer and would be likely to break when driven into hardwoods.

4 Drill the pilot holes for the remaining screws.

5 Now insert the remaining screws. It looks much neater if all the slots are in line or on the same diagonal.

6 When the box closes, the faces should meet with no more than the clearance of a thin piece of paper to allow for the thickness of a coating of lacquer at the finishing stage. If the hinge recesses have been accurately marked to start with (see MEASURING AND LAYING OUT) and then cut out with care, perfect alignment should result. Note that the hinge knuckles protrude slightly.

7 Any fractional misalignment can be sanded down with a sanding block on the front and side edges to bring them level.

Inserting a mortise lock

1 The various recessed parts of the lock need to be marked and cut in stages. First place the lock on the wood to mark its overall outline.

2 The marks are squared across with a combination square and marking knife in a similar manner to marking the hinges.

3 Use the adjustable-depth try-square facility of the combination square to extend the lines downward.

4 Use a tenon or dovetail saw to cut across the grain to the line on the side and edge.

5 Mark the various features of the lock by holding it against the wood.

6 For the shallow recess, chisel out the waste horizontally across the grain.

7 In such a confined space, the trickiest part is to cut an accurate line along the grain at the bottom of the lock. Here the bevel of the chisel is used to give a vertical cut.

Keyhole location

1 Mark out the keyhole position using a marking gauge and try square to transfer the information from the lock.

2 Drill a slightly oversized hole for the keyhole. Using a coping saw, insert the blade into the hole, then carefully cut the keyhole verticals, finally trimming with a narrow chisel.

3 Now insert the lock into its recess and check that everything is flush. In this confined space, use a nail with its tip flattened as a screw pilot hole.

4 Attach the lock with fine screws, and check the key for operation when the catch plate has been attached.

5 The catch has to be very accurately recessed into the lid so that the key operates smoothly. The catch will sit flush (level with the wood) in the lid. Mark its profile with a try square and marking gauge.

6 Recess the catch using the same methods as used for recessing the hinges.

7 Drill pilot holes and attach with fine screws, ensuring everything is perfectly flush.

8 A fine bevel can be run along the edge with a smoothing plane as a continuation of the hinge bevel for visual effect.

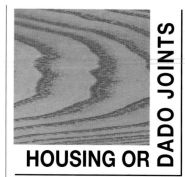

HOUSING OR DADO JOINTS

The housing or dado joint, is a strong, simple, joint in which a groove is cut across the grain of one piece of wood into which another piece is fitted. The joint is usually found in cabinet construction for shelves and dividers in furniture such as dressers or bookcases.

In its simplest form, the housing or dado joint consists of a shallow-bottomed groove running the full width of the

wood, into which the square-edged piece sits. Variations of the joint include stopped shoulders – where the groove doesn't run the full width of the wood, so the joint is not visible from the front – and dovetailed sectioned grooves for maximum mechanical strength, which are nowadays most often cut with a router.

Housings or dados which go along the grain rather than across it, such as in drawer making, are similar in construction but tend to be much narrower because of the thinness of material used in drawer bottoms.

The joint is normally glued, and in crude constructions pins or screws can be used to re-inforce it; the groove prevents the pin or screw from splitting narrow-section wood and gives the joint added grip.

There are various ways to make housing or dado joints by hand, power tool, or machine, such as using jigged-tool-guiding blocks (see JIGS AND JIGMAKING), or with saws and chisels or by cutting with a radial-arm saw (see SAWING). You will find that power tools are much quicker and usually more accurate, but hand skills are well worth developing for your own satisfaction as a craftsperson.

CHECKLIST

Marking knife or pencil
Try square
Steel ruler or straightedge
Marking gauge
2 "C" clamps
Batten

Tenon saw
Paring chisel and/or router plane

Small electric router
Straight fence
Straight bit
Dovetail bit

See pages 8-9

Making a through housing or dado joint by hand

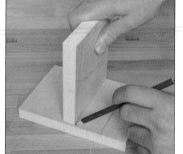

1 Cut the wood accurately to size (see SQUARING WOOD). Mark the position of the joint on the piece to be grooved by tracing thickness marks onto it using a marking knife, pencil, or ballpoint pen.

2 Extend the lines across the wood using a large try square or by extending the reach of a standard one by placing a straight-edge next to it (see MEASURING AND LAYING OUT).

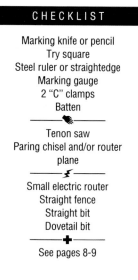

6 Remove the waste with a chisel and mallet. The fibers should break away quite easily as they are weak across the grain where they have been severed lengthwise by the saw.

7 By using the bevel of the chisel tip, you can cut in further without the handle rubbing the wood, but this takes a little more skill. This is because there is less of the tool in contact with the wood, which makes it harder to control.

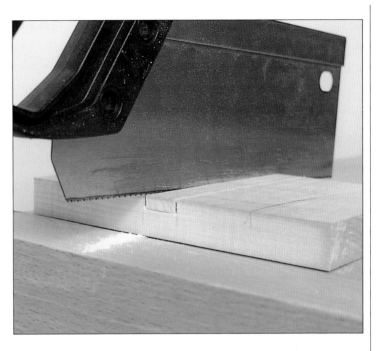

3 Now extend lines to about one, third of the thickness of the wood with the try square on the other face, to give you the depth of the groove to be cut (this one-third is a general rule). Set a marking gauge and mark the line on both ends of the piece. Shade in the waste to show clearly which part has to be removed.

4 Secure the wood to the bench with one or two "C" clamps and use a tenon saw to cut the walls of the housing or dado joint to the line. For extra control you can use both hands on the saw handle. Try it each way and see which is best.

5 The saw should cut just on the waste side of the line, leaving the thickness of the line intact. This will give you a nice snug fit (see JOINTS).

8 Now turn the wood around and chisel in from the other side (see CHISELING), working down to the bottom of the housing or dado joint in a series of fine cuts.

9 Alternatively you can use a router plane with its adjustable-hooked cutter. Set it to depth each time to make a series of ⅛-inch cuts. The wood fibers break up easily.

10 The advantage of using a router plane is that it levels the bottom of the housing or dado joint perfectly because the base of the plane sits on the surface of the wood on each side of the groove, thus making it impossible to cut too deeply if the cutter is set to the correct depth. You may wish to combine the methods by first removing the bulk of the waste quickly with a chisel and mallet.

11 Plane a fractional bevel on the end of the other piece to create a "leading edge" for ease of entry and "persuade" the two pieces together using a hammer and piece of scrapwood to avoid any bruising. Make sure the ends are flush.

Making a dovetailed stopped housing or dado joint with an electric router

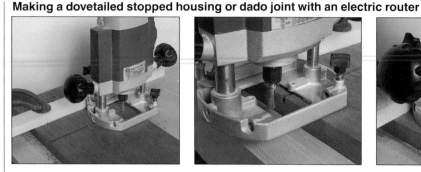

  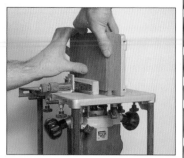

1 The dovetailed housing or dado joint is cut in stages, using a straight bit and then a dovetail bit to prolong the life of both. This eases the path of the more bulky dovetail cutter and thus reduces its workload. It is impossible to lower the dovetail bit in a series of shallow cuts because of its shape. It must always be introduced into the wood from the side.

First set up a plunge router with a small straight bit. Then clamp a batten to the wood to serve as a guide. The router is placed on the wood, the bit in line with the groove, and the batten is clamped tight against the side of the router. Mark with a pencil where the groove stops. Now rout a series of shallow stepped cuts down to almost full depth.

2 Replace the straight bit with the appropriately sized dovetail bit, setting the depth-stop so that the bit achieves the full profiled cut in one pass. You can now see that because the bulk of the waste has been removed more gently with the straight bit, the dovetail bit can open up the desired profile.

3 Carefully rout out the dovetailed housing or dado joint in one pass, being sure to keep the router pressed tight against the batten. Do not be tempted to release the plunge mechanism at the end of the cut, but withdraw the bit back along its own path. For wider-sectioned dovetailed housing or dado joint, place a thin strip next to the batten so that a second cut can be made next to the first.

4 You will find that the best way to fashion the dovetailed shoulders of the other piece is to set the router upside down in a router table, using the same bit. Router tables are quite cheap to buy, and you will find that they increase the scope of a router tremendously. Set the adjustments for depth and width of cut. The wood is passed through to cut one side and then the other.

5 Now remove the stopped portion by first sawing down the grain with a tenon or dovetail saw (see SAWING) and then across the grain. The stopped portion, remember, has to be cut away, because in this case the groove on the other piece did not go right across the full width of the wood. For proper control, make sure the wood is firm in the vice and adjusted so that each sawing operation is executed vertically.

6 Because the end of the dovetailed housing or dado joint is curved to follow the bit shape, you have to round off the end of the joint to match. This is simply done with a sharp chisel.

7 Carefully slide the two pieces together ready for gluing. There is a tendency for wide panels to warp, making it difficult to withdraw "dry" joints, so gluing should be done as soon as possible (see GLUING).

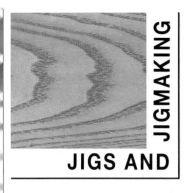

JIGS AND JIGMAKING

A jig is a device used to hold or guide the wood while it is being worked on, or to hold or guide the tool being used often for repeat actions. The craft of woodworking becomes an art when you start making your own jigs.

Once you have acquired the basic woodworking techniques of measuring, sawing, chiseling, planing, etc., and can make joints fit the first time (see JOINTS), you will soon see that much woodworking is either based on repeat operations (such as fashioning identical members) or dealing with awkward "one-off" problems which standardized equipment and methods do not readily solve.

Behind the art of jigmaking is the ability to improvise, and for many trained woodworkers it often means putting aside a rather rigid doctrine and thinking "laterally," using whatever means are available. Jigs can be very simple or sometimes really quite complex. They are usually the brainchild of the individual and more often than not are quite simple solutions for very specific applications. This might mean the use of pins and nails, tape, a hot-melt glue gun (as an extra pair of hands), cutoffs of

plywood, particle board, and MDF, and quick solidifying materials such as car body filler.

Certain hand and power tools require jigs for specific tasks, either to make the task easier or quicker.

CHECKLIST

MDF, particle board, or plywood
Softwood
Hot-melt glue gun
Screws, nails, brads
Masking tape
A range of hand tools
A range of power tools
See pages 8-9

Some basic jigs for hand tools

 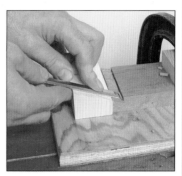

1 A custom-built saw guide is used here for cutting dovetail dados or housings. A thick block of wood is sawn and planed accurately and when "C" clamped to the wood it acts as a guide for the saw blade. Care has to be taken in aligning the jig perfectly with the wall of the housing or dado.

2 An angled block can help maintain a consistent and accurate cut when chiseling the corresponding piece to a dovetailed housing or dado joint.

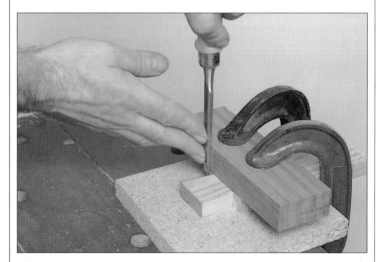

3 Similarly a square-edged hardwood block can be used for trimming the shoulder lines of a dovetail with a chisel. The block should be clamped perfectly in line with the shoulder line and the chisel pressed firmly against the vertical wall of the block.

Using a dowel-cutting jig

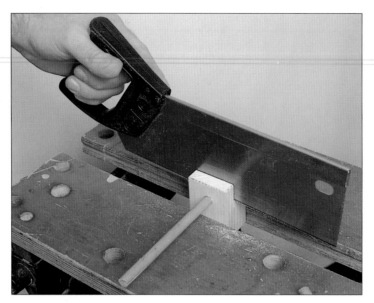

1 One of the simplest workshop jigs to make is this dowel-cutting device – a small block of wood with a hole, a saw cut, and a nail partially buried.

2 First, support the jig in the vice. Bevel the end of a piece of dowel and push it through till it is flush with the other side. Now insert a tenon saw in the saw cut and cut through the dowel.

3 Using a hammer, drive the dowel through the end. As it passes against the nail point, a groove is formed which acts as an air escape channel in the dowel joint. This also allows excess glue to escape.

Simple power-tool jigs

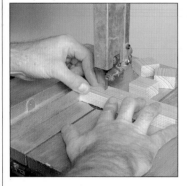

1 The bandsaw (see SAWING) is an ideal powered tool for jigging up. The most basic jig is its standard straight fence which can be used for parallel repeat cuts along or across the grain.

2 Saw kerfing can be achieved easily on the bandsaw by mounting a straight-edged scrap piece on the saw table with "C" clamps so that the blade is half-buried in a saw cut. This acts as a sawing depth-stop. With a push stick, you can make a series of cuts, aligning the previous cut with a mark on the straight piece of equal spacing.

3 The router is perhaps the most versatile power tool for work with jigs (see ROUTING). Indeed the router body is a jig for guiding the path of the bit. Here is a simple method of trimming the ends of dovetail or milled joints. Attach a thin piece of ply or MDF to the joint piece with masking tape or "C" clamps.

4 Position the MDF just behind the shoulder line of the dovetails. The MDF serves as a spacer for accurately setting the depth of the bit to the surface of the wood while operating the router sole against the MDF.

A simple wheel-cutting device

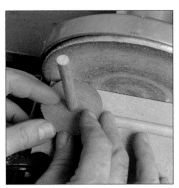

1 This simple device – designed by the author – is used to cut accurate wheels for toys or other small circular sections which require a center hole. It consists of a block of wood with a groove cut into it. It is mounted onto a disk sander table.

2 An oversize "wheel" is roughly cut on the bandsaw, and its spindle fits loosely in the groove. As the wheel is rotated against the abrading disk, pressure of the dowel spindle is increased against the inside wall of the groove.

3 First a small "flat" is sanded against the marked circle on the wheel, which is cut slightly oversize.

4 Insert the wheel with its spindle protruding into the groove against the outer edge of the groove. Using finger control, slowly rotate the wheel so that it makes contact with the sanding disk and abrades gradually to the line. Take care not to catch your fingers on the sanding disk as it rotates. Any number of wheels can be made; try it!

Jigmaking materials

MDF, particle board, a hot-melt glue gun, and pins or screws are ideal partners for jigmaking. You can quickly build custom jigs which need to be only as permanent as the job at hand.

Making a jig for the planer-thicknesser

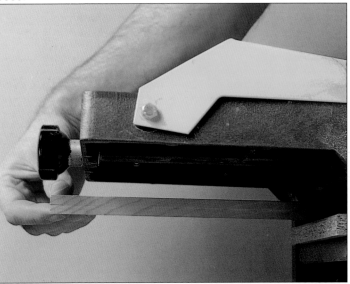

1 A taper channel is constructed by gluing and pinning the corresponding waste pieces onto the particle board. A stop underneath secures the jig to the thicknessing table.

2 The tapered piece is planed down in the thicknesser in stages until the required taper is formed.

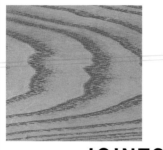

JOINTS

Jointing is at the very heart of woodworking. It is, arguably, the most important technique to learn, as well as being a very satisfying experience when done well. Most woodworking consists of joining pieces of wood together for a variety of purposes – be it for changing shape, creating structure, maximizing strength, or dealing with wood movement.

There is the decorative aspect, too: when two pieces of wood join, they create immense visual interest (sometimes even mystery).

There are hundreds of joints in existence. Many have evolved over the centuries to meet specific functional requirements, such as the MORTISE-AND-TENON and DOVETAIL JOINTS in frame and carcass construction. As such, joints embody a rich and long-standing wood culture, and – just as a particular wood such as oak spans entire centuries and thus has strong historical associations – so too do particular wood joints, most notably the dovetail.

Joints and wood movement

Not least in importance in the vast vocabulary of wood joints is the behavior of wood itself, namely wood movement. This is something all woodworkers must reckon with because nature will get its way.

Wood is like a sponge, absorbing, holding, and losing moisture from the air. All joints therefore move to a degree, and their geometry and dimensions are crucial factors in restricting or coping with wood movement. A well-designed joint is strong, visually attractive, or cleverly hidden and, above all, survives the passage of time, when constant shrinking and swelling of the fibers affect its structure.

A simple rule is that wood tends to move across the grain rather than along the grain, and the annual rings (visible on end grain) will try to straighten out. Therefore be careful to select wood which is quarter-sawn (with short annual rings across the board section); this will minimize wood movement.

Modern "permanent" adhesives have given a degree of freedom in jointing methods. A thin VENEER glued down with a modern glue is unlikely to shrink and split, but a thick panel glued to another with incorrect grain intersections will move. It is not the glue line which breaks, but the wood fibers around it.

Jointing manufactured boards

Manufactured boards such as particle board and MDF are less prone to wood movement, and hence employ a different variety of connecting methods. Board materials anyway have little localized mechanical strength and break away at the edges if traditional solid wood joints are used.

These materials exploit modern machine jointing methods such as grooved splines or designated milled joint bits (see EDGE-JOINTING). The subject of jointing manmade boards is very wide, and it would be safe to say that if your particular interest in woodworking lies in this field, further reading will be necessary.

The principles of wood jointing

There is nothing more satisfying than to cut a tight joint, as it demands not only an understanding of the nature of the material, but a good command of technique with a keen eye and sustained concentration. Some understanding of the principles of wood jointing helps before acquiring the "knacks" of how to make a tight joint. A basic rule is to avoid short grain. If a joint is cut too close to the end of a piece of wood and the fibers are severed deeper across the grain than along it, the stress of the joint and any leverage bearing upon it will result in the "short grain" breaking along the grain.

COMMON JOINTS

- **Butt joint:** simple carcassing; useful if no real strength is needed.

- **Half lap joint:** for joining wood of the same section at an angle.

- **Tongue-and-groove:** for joining boards edgeways; useful in paneling.

- **Spline joint:** similar to tongue-and-groove, but with a loose spline.

- **Mortise-and-tenon:** one of the most common framing joints; consists of a square hole with a square peg in it.

- **Dovetail:** comes in many forms, some hidden; common in carcassing and drawer-making; often used overtly to show quality and craftsmanship.

- **Scarf:** used to join two pieces of wood lengthwise; often used in shipbuilding.

- **Dowel joint:** an easy alternative to the mortise-and-tenon; can be surprisingly difficult to align; useful in cabinetmaking.

- **Biscuit joint:** a modern technique used largely for edge-jointing, but useful in other areas.

- **Miter:** popular with picture framers, cabinetmakers etc., but with no inherent strength; invariably needs reinforcement of some kind.

X-Y RULE ON JOINTS

When cutting a joint close to the end of a piece of wood, the depth of the cut ("X") must not exceed the length of the piece remaining on the end ("Y"). If it does, this short grain will certainly break. This is because the pressure or leverage to which the joint is subjected is too great for the short grain over the reduced area.

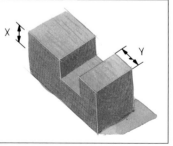

Principles of wood jointing – a basic guide

1 An end-grain-to-end-grain glue joint (see GLUING) is the weakest, as there is no fiber overlap and the glue is absorbed down the grain, leaving too little on the matching surfaces.

2 An end-grain-to-side-grain glue joint is almost as weak as **1** above for the same reasons and also because the wood will shrink across the grain and stress the glue line.

3 The strongest glue joint occurs when two similar grain directions meet side by side, in effect continuing the figure of the wood. When shrinkage occurs, it is consistent as both pieces behave in the same way (see EDGE-JOINTING).

4 By introducing a shoulder to the joint, it becomes mechanically stronger and the principle of strong jointing is to create maximum fiber overlap and maximum glue area. Here you can see the dovetail and milled joints are mechanically strong. They also offer great visual interest.

Types of joint configuration

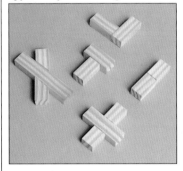  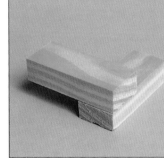

1 There are basically four jointing configurations to be found in wood constructions: "L," "T," "X," and "I." There are also oblique or angled variations of these types. Each configuration can be achieved by a variety of joints. For instance, the "L" type can be a HALVING OR LAP joint, a MITER joint, a bridle joint, a DOWEL joint, a DOVETAIL joint or a MORTISE-AND-TENON. Hence the family of joints is extensive.

2 This is the simplest "L" joint, in which one piece overlaps the other with adjacent grain and the glue bond is reasonably strong. Such a joint could either be nailed or screwed together. It can be made stronger by setting one piece into the other, creating a shoulder which helps lock the two pieces together. When the shoulder is cut halfway through the thickness of each piece, a HALVING OR LAP joint results which is the strongest type of glued "L" joint.

3 On the left is shown an "L" miter joint, and you can see that the same two pieces of wood can be rearranged to form other joint types – an oblique scarf joint and a normal scarf joint (both variations of an "I" configuration).

The knack of making tight joints

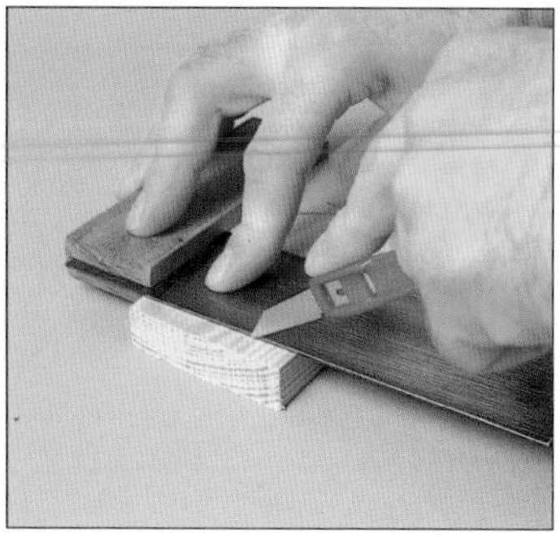

1 Tight joints rely on care and accuracy in initial laying out (see MEASURING AND LAYING OUT). First, your choice of marking instrument is vital, depending on the scale and nature of work. For precision cabinet work, a marking knife makes the most accurate line. Hold it like a pen with index finger pressing down. Draw the blade across at a shallow angle, close to the measuring tool, such as a try square. Make sure the square is squeezed firmly against the wood.

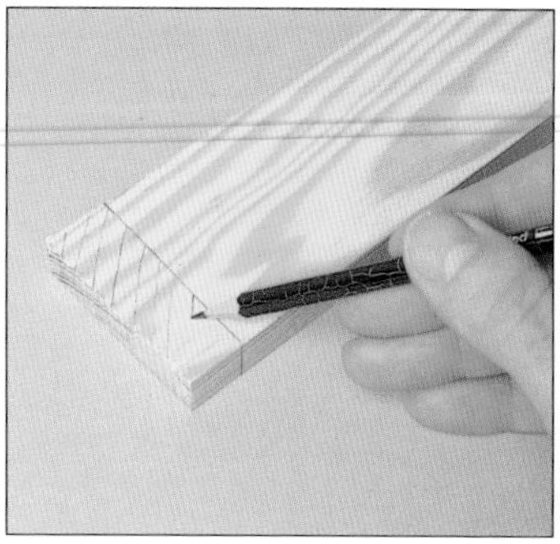

2 Clearly shade waste areas (those to be cut away). The most effective is diagonal shading because it is visibly arresting, and should be done with a medium/ soft leaded pencil.

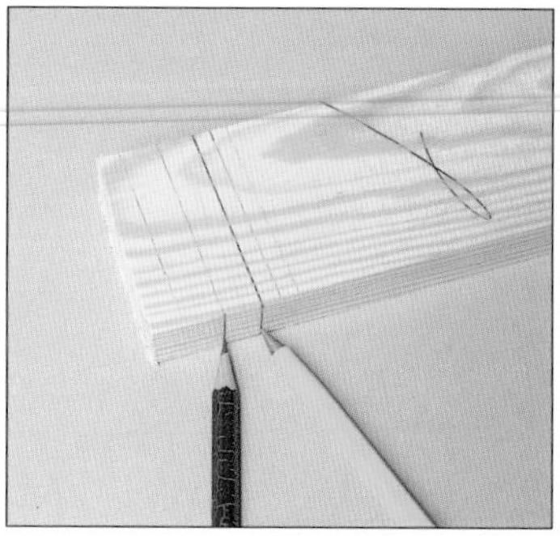

3 Many woodworkers use a pencil for laying out. Ideally a hard-leaded pencil gives the most accurate line, but it is difficult to see, whereas a soft-leaded one is bolder but blunts as it draws, which affects accuracy. A good example is when a line is "squared" around the wood: where the lines meet, the two pencil thicknesses are apparent. An effective modern marking tool is a ballpoint pen, which leaves a bold and consistent line.

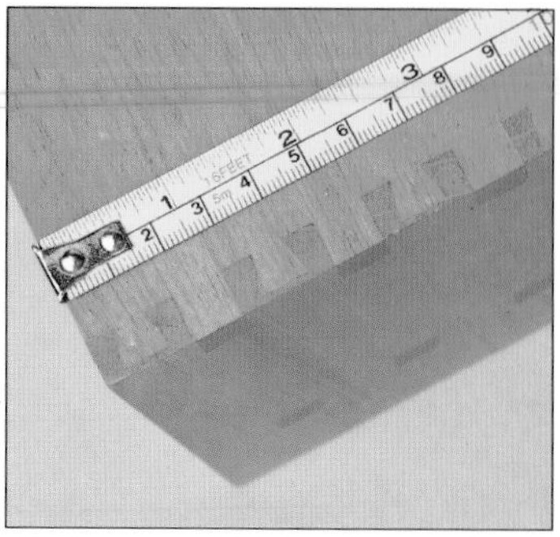

4 A tape measure is useful in woodworking generally, but it must be remembered that it is not the most accurate method of measuring. The hook is loose and often graduations are inaccurate to ⅛ inch over a 3-foot length. You would not use a tape measure to mark out these tiny and precise joints (a dovetail variation designed by the author).

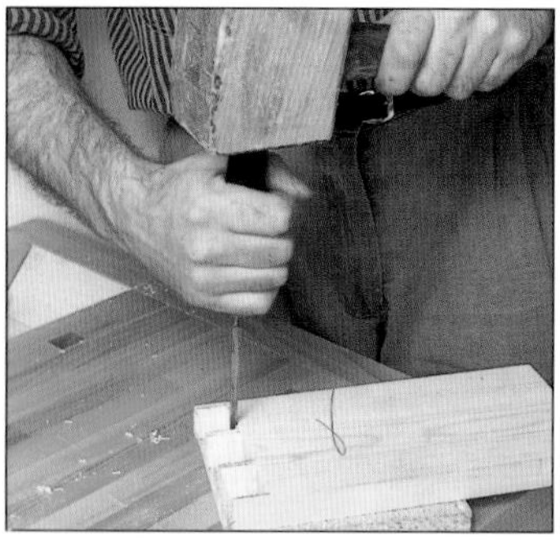

9 The final chisel cut is made by placing the tip of the chisel exactly on the line and very carefully removing the last portion of waste (see DOVETAIL JOINTS). Successful joint cutting (indeed all woodworking) also relies on the way you stand and hold tools.

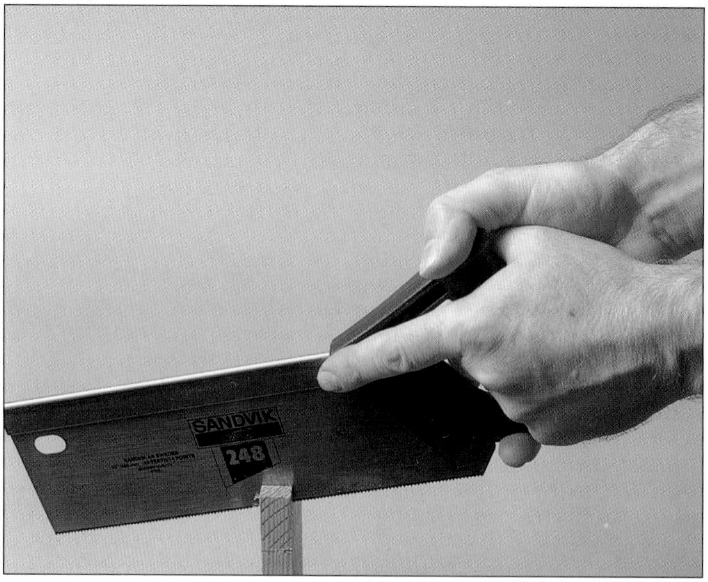

10 When using a tenon saw, far greater control can be achieved by using both hands. There is twice the power, and both elbows act as pivots, forcing correct alignment of the body and in particular, the eye, with the line to be cut (see SAWING).

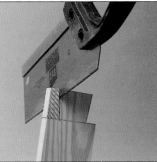

5 A steel ruler gives the best accuracy, and in fine woodworking you need to be able to measure in $1/64$-inch increments. Mark with a marking knife rather than a pencil as the latter will not be precise enough.

6 A tight joint relies on the springiness or "give" of the wood, so you obviously need to make the joint slightly tight, but by how much is hard to quantify, especially as the variable factors are the size of the joint and the character and hardness of the wood. However a guide is that, in a medium-density hardwood, the joint might be about $1/64$ inch oversize. A tiny bevel or "leading edge" helps ease the joint together.

7 A crucial factor is where on the line to make the saw cut. This is where the "$1/64$-inch" rule makes sense because you do not actually measure it, but instead you place the saw on the line, or just off it, so that the line is left after sawing. This is the knack of cutting a tight joint. The line therefore serves as a cutting reference point.

8 This rule applies to lines marked and cut down the grain, in which the springiness of the wood is a factor, but for lines marked across the grain, for example shoulder lines on joints, the cutaway portion is usually made right on the line. This is generally why shoulder lines are marked with a marking knife.

A totally mechanical joint
This is an ingenious Japanese joint called a "Kanawa-tsugi" or mortised rabbeted oblique scarf joint. It is a challenge for any woodworker to make (this one is by the author) as it is an exercise in laying out and cutting. The intricate overlapping cutaway portions are tightly interlocked by a slightly tapered wedge, driving the two pieces together. When withdrawn, the two pieces come apart. No glue is used, and therefore this is a totally mechanical joint offering maximum strength. It also emphasizes the visual honesty of joints – the structure is the esthetic.

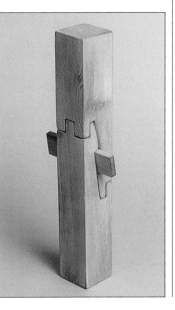

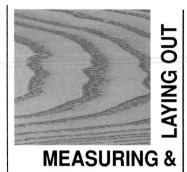

MEASURING & LAYING OUT

It is very rare in woodworking to take the tools straight to the material without first marking the wood or setting everything out. Precision is crucial for accurate working. This may be acceptable for a tomato box – accurate perhaps to ⅛ inch or so – but not for a piece of cabinetry for which accuracy may need to be as fine as 1/64 inch or even less. Often mistakes made later in the making of a piece can be attributed to poor measuring and laying out.

The simplest measuring is achieved with a measuring stick (any flat and straight piece of wood), and marks can be transferred from one piece of wood to another, such as the identical lengths of table legs. Indeed after the initial measurement has been taken with a calibrated rule, it is often more accurate to copy subsequent components from the original which in effect becomes the "measuring stick."

Some woodworking joints are measured out on one piece first, cut with the saw and chisel, then copied onto the other piece (see DOVETAIL JOINTS), whereas other joints are marked independently for maximum accuracy (see MORTISE-AND-TENON JOINTS).

Choice of marker

What is crucial to accurate laying out, whether you use a measuring stick, steel ruler, or other aids, is the choice of marker. Effective laying out is bold and precise, and the areas to be cut away as "waste" are shaded clearly. Traditionally, woodworkers use a pencil or marking knife; increasingly, ballpoint pens are used.

A pencil tends to blunt as it draws which makes a wider and less accurate line (unless it is a hard pencil and then it can be difficult to see the mark). A marking knife gives the most accurate results, but leaves an incised mark, difficult to remove afterward and allowing no margin of error for beginners.

The most fundamental rule of all in measuring and marking is to check, check, and check again.

CHECKLIST

Pencil, ballpoint pen, marking knife
Try square
Steel ruler
Tape measure
Measuring stick(s)
Marking gauge
Combination square
Miter square
Sliding bevel
Mortise gauge
Trammel
Pair of compasses
Center square

+

See pages 8-9

Measuring and marking parallel lines

1 There are various ways to measure and mark parallel lines. The easiest is to use a tape measure, stepping off two marks at each end of the board. But you can also use a steel ruler or measuring sticks.

2 A steel straightedge or steel ruler can be used to mark a line across the two measured points. Spread your fingers along the straight-edge to ensure it does not slip. Mark the line up to the edge of the ruler.

Measuring to length

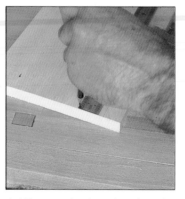 

1 When cutting boards to length (see SQUARING WOOD) it is always best to start off with a fresh "squared" edge. Measure in with the rule about ¼in to square the first line across. (This is the minimum distance for sawing without the fibers disintegrating, and when this happens control of the saw is very difficult.)

2 Set the zero at the ¼in mark and measure off the required dimension, spreading the fingers again to keep the steel rule steady.

Squaring lines

1 A marking knife and try square are used to square the lines across. The marking knife is more accurate, although a pencil can be used.

2 When using a try square (which is fixed at exactly 90 degrees), always squeeze the stock against the edge of the wood, using all fingers. Carefully score a line with the knife tight against the steel blade of the square.

3 Extend the line all the way around the wood, using the try square against the face side and face edge with their respective reference marks.

Shading/duplicating lengths

Waste is traditionally shaded with a pencil and, when two or more pieces are to be cut, spacing lines are drawn for the saw thickness. Duplicate lengths are easily measured by using a measuring device such as abrasive paper.

Laying out a row of dovetails

1 Here we show how dovetails can be accurately layed out; this technique can be applied to any panel where equal divisions are required. Equal divisions can be stepped off by using a tape measure diagonally. With both edges of the wood, line up the chosen graduations and step off the intervals. Use a try square against the end of the piece of wood to extend these marks parallel to the sides to meet the end.

2 On the wood, mark a shoulder line the thickness of the other piece of wood. Then use a dovetail template and steel ruler to mark the dovetail pitch. To do this step off ⅛-inch marks on each side of each vertical line, and align the template and mark each dovetail. Shade in the waste afterward.

3 As a general rule, an extra $\frac{1}{32}$ inch should be added to the distance of joint shoulder lines to allow for cleaning up afterward. If the shoulder line is exactly the same thickness as the wood, the thickness of that wood has to be planed under size when cleaning the joint up.

Using other marking squares

1 A miter square can be used like a try square, but for fixed 45 degree angles. Here both tools are used to mark alternately all the way around the wood.

2 A combination square is a versatile tool with a sliding straight-edge. It can be used as a try square or miter square.

3 The length of the straightedge (which is also a ruler) can be adjusted to suit the task.

4 Here the combination square is being used as a simple gauge for penciling parallel lines.

Using a marking gauge

1 A marking gauge is used for marking parallel lines. Its adjustable stock is secured to the stem with a screw. A pointed spur makes the mark. A steel ruler is used to measure the setting, then the gauge is used very firmly against the edge of the wood.

2 You can hold the wood in the vice or support it against a bench stop when using a marking gauge.

3 A quick way to set a marking gauge to the center of a piece of wood is to first set the gauge by guessing, then step off a mark from each side. Finally intersect the marks with the spur and set. Fine adjustments can be made by banging the locked gauge against the benchtop to move the stock fractionally along the stem.

Using a mortise gauge

The practice of knocking a gauge for fine setting should not be used on a mortise gauge which has a brass double spur adjuster. The two spurs are set to the width of a mortise chisel (see MORTISE-AND-TENON JOINTS) and then the stock is set to the appropriate position by repeating the centering method.

Marking circles and radii

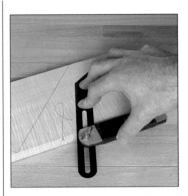

5 A sliding bevel can be adjusted to any angle for measuring work. Here again, the stock should be held firmly against the edge of the wood.

6 The sliding bevel can mark or check both external and internal angles. It is tightened by a screw or wing nut.

Mark circles and radii with compasses, first use them to step off the center mark from adjacent edges.

Other marking operations

1 It is easy to make a trammel for scribing small and large curves. One end is drilled to take a ballpoint pen and a brad is used as a center point at the required measured distance.

2 Finding the center of circular pieces of wood such as turnery blanks (see TURNING WOOD) can be achieved with a workshop-made center square. Two adjacent positions give a cross. Slightly irregular circles can be marked by stepping off a series of random marks around the circumference.

3 Measuring sticks are immensely useful in woodworking. Here two small cutoffs are used to accurately measure internal lengths. The sticks are overlapped and a mark placed across them.

4 The importance of coding pieces of work not only helps minimize confusion when re-arranging several identical pieces, but their exact positions can be easily marked ready for gluing and assembly (see GLUING).

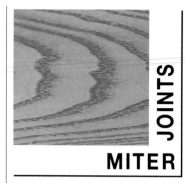

MITER JOINTS

A miter joint consists of two pieces with their ends cut at 45 degrees which meet to form a right angle. A typical example is the corner of a picture frame, but the joint can also apply to the corner of a carcass.

On its own the miter joint has no strength because the mating surfaces don't interlock, they simply butt against each other. For this reason it is usually glued with some kind of reinforcement such as an internal tongue (see BISCUIT JOINTS), or pins, dowels, or veneer inserts. Because there is no visible end grain, the joint offers some advantages; it is

CHECKLIST

Miter square or combination square
Try square
Steel ruler
Masking tape or "C" clamps
Hot-melt glue gun

Tenon saw, dovetail saw, or
Gentleman's saw
Smoothing plane

Table saw

See pages 8-9

both visually pleasing and particularly suitable in constructions in which grooves can be later cut straight through to align in adjacent boards, or for continuous edge profiles.

The glue area of a miter joint is curiously neither "end grain" nor "side grain" (see JOINTS), but tends to follow the characteristics of end grain, absorbing the glue and not forming a very strong bond.

On large-sectioned miter joints, the glue line tends to open up after a period of time, no matter how accurately the joint has been made. This is due to shrinkage, or expansion.

The miter joint can be cut with a handsaw, by various powered saws and also by special guillotines.

VARIOUS MITER USES

Miter joints are used for frames and carcasses and are usually reinforced to stop them from breaking.

A typical way of reinforcing a miter is with dowels. In this case accurate alignment is extremely important.

The miter is ideal for shaped edges or grooves to be run continuously from one part of the joint to another.

Making a miter joint by hand

1 Cut the wood to size (see SQUARING WOOD). Use a miter square to mark the 45-degree angles on both pieces.

Extend the vertical lines using a try square. It is not always necessary to mark the line all the way around the wood, especially on thin-sectioned wood.

2 Place the wood on a bench-hook or clamp it to the bench using a "C" clamp with the end extending over the benchtop. Use a tenon saw to cut to the line (see SAWING). Repeat the operation on the other piece, taking care to saw on the waste side of the line and checking the saw cut is vertical.

Check the joint aligns perfectly, using a try square, and trim with a handplane if necessary. Keep to the marked line as this is the only accurate guide.

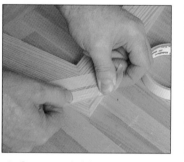

3 One way of gluing the miter joint together is to use masking tape to stretch across the glue line. You first stretch a piece of tape across the center, then add more strips and repeat the process, carefully turning the wood over to the other side to equalize the pressure. Masking tape is an underrated woodworking aid.

4 Alternatively two 45-degree blocks can be attached with a hot-melt glue gun to serve as temporary clamping blocks and chiseled off afterward. It is important to line up the clamp with the center of the glue line to obtain even pressure.

Making a frame miter joint using a table saw

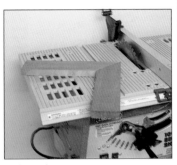

1 Set up the table saw so that the blade height clears above the thickness of the wood to be cut. Set the sliding miter fence "manually" by using a parallel piece of wood carefully set between saw teeth (note arrow marks) and a miter square. Never rely on the calibrations of the machine, as this allows too much room for error.

2 Having cut the wood to the required size, lower the saw blade guard into position, place the wood against the miter fence to overlap the line of the saw blade, grip the wood firmly against the miter fence, and pass it slowly across the saw blade, keeping fingers well away from the blade. *(Machine guard has been taken off for clarity of illustration.)*

3 The other piece is sawn in the same way to make the miter joint. The table saw can also be used with its parallel fence set so that a reinforced "loose tongue" (see EDGE-JOINTING) can be grooved along the mitered ends of the wood. Lower the saw blade and test the method on a scrap piece first (see SAWING).

Making a veneer reinforced "picture frame" miter joint

1 This method is particularly suitable for small-sectioned wood frames. Make the miter joint by hand- or power-tool methods and glue it together. When dry, mount the joint in the vice and use a miter square and pencil to mark a diagonal line to indicate the base line of the sawn veneer inserts. Then use a marking gauge to mark two lines dividing the thickness into thirds.

2 On a scrap piece of wood, try out a saw cut using a tenon saw, dovetail saw, or gentleman's saw to match the thickness of the cut to a selected piece of thick veneer (beech or ash). When you have established a suitable saw kerf (see SAWING), carefully cut down the marked lines on the wood.

3 Now insert the veneer into the saw cuts, trace around it, and using a marking knife and steel ruler, carefully cut the veneer slightly oversize, ready for gluing.

4 Glue the veneer inserts into the saw cuts using white or yellow glue, spreading it liberally over all surfaces. Carefully slide the veneers into the saw cuts and leave to dry for at least 2 hours. Finally clean up the joint using a smoothing plane and/or sandpaper block.

MORTISE & TENON JOINTS

The mortise-and-tenon – easily identified by its "tongue" and "mouth" components – is probably the most common woodworking joint. Being widely used for doors and frames over the years, its place is firmly entrenched in history.

It was originally a "dry" joint, often held together with wooden pegs before the advent of glues, and therefore is predominantly a mechanical joint – even when

---

CHECKLIST

Marking knife, pencil, or ballpoint pen
Steel ruler
Try square
Mortise gauge
Tenon saw
Hammer and scrapwood block
Marking gauge
———✎———
¼-inch mortise chisel
Mallet
½-inch beveled edge chisel
Smoothing plane
———✗———
Powered mortiser
½-inch mortising bit
Radial-arm saw with tungsten-carbide tipped (TCT) blade
———✦———
See pages 8-9

---

the glue breaks down, as it does in many old pieces, the joint still works (see JOINTS).

The mortise-and-tenon family
The mortise-and-tenon refers to a family of joints, and the most basic one is the through mortise-and-tenon, which offers maximum strength as the "tongue" extends to the full depth of the "mouth." The hidden "stub tenon" joint penetrates to about two-thirds the width of the wood. It is these two particular joints which we look at in detail here, although there are very many variations. Long- and short-shouldered mortise-and-tenons accommodate rabbets on one face. Haunch mortise-and-tenons are used in corner frames of wide sections to deter warping.

Bare-faced tenons have no shoulders and are therefore quicker to make, but in general a shoulder all the way around offers better anchorage and conceals the tricky part of making, which is the fit of the tenon in the mortise.

The mortise-and-tenon can be cut by hand- or power-tool methods, particularly the tenon which in essence is a double-rabbeted member. As a framework corner joint ("L" configuration), the haunch mortise-and-tenon is a useful joint to make and varies in detail from the technique of making a through mortise-and-tenon for a "T" configuration.

Cutting a through mortise-and-tenon by hand

1 Cut the wood to size (see SQUARING WOOD). Then mark the shoulder lines on the tenon to correspond with the width of the wood. Leave 1/32 inch for cleaning up afterward. Then mark two lines across the mortise piece to correspond with the width of the tenon minus 1/32 inch for cleaning up afterward. Place code marks "A" on the wood for clarity.

2 As the tenon goes all the way through the other piece, the mortise has to be marked on both edges, so extend the marks to the other edge using a try square with its stock held against the face on the waste side of the line down the tenon faces.

A BASIC MORTISE AND TENON AND A HAUNCHED VARIATION

The basic mortise-and-tenon is a simple joint where the square tenon (tongue) fits snugly into the mortise (mouth). This common joint has been used in furniture-making for centuries in this, the most elementary form.

A haunched mortise-and-tenon is a variation which involves the addition of an extra part designed to give strength if the joint is used on the corners of frames.

3 A double-spurred mortise gauge is used to mark the corresponding tenon and mortise width; usually this is about one-third of the thickness of the wood. In this case the wood is ¾ inch thick and ¼-inch mortise chisel is used – they come in sizes of ¼, ⅜ and ½ inch. Set the spurs slightly wider than the chisel width.

4 Now set the stock of the gauge so that the spurs centralize across the thickness of the wood and gauge the lines using the stock against the face side. Gauge both edges.

5 Mount the tenon piece in the vice and carefully use the gauge with the same setting to correspond with the mortise. The laying out is now completed.

6 Mount the wood firmly on the bench in line with a leg. The best way to do this is to use a piece of scrapwood in the vice, then clamp the wood to it. Stand at the end of the bench in line with the mortise. Using the chisel and mallet, make a series of fine cuts at ⅛-inch intervals from the center toward each end. Use a try square to guide the alignment of the chisel.

7 A waste portion is needed for leveraging the chips out, so do not chisel right up to the line. The depth of cut of the mallet stroke is about ¼ inch each time, depending on the type of wood. In hardwoods you may have to take a little less than this.
Now carefully leverage the chips out. Repeat this process in staged depths.

8 You can see how the chisel pivots on the waste area left when removing the chips. After you have cut through to about halfway, reverse the wood and repeat the action.

9 When re-mounting the wood, take care to clear debris from the benchtop as it can dent the finished work.

10 Now stand in front of the bench and carefully chisel the mortise end walls vertically. A try square helps align the cut. It is important the ends are flat and square. As the mortise gauge was set slightly over the thickness of the chisel, a fractional amount is now left for paring with a wider chisel. This is to ensure the mortise side walls are perfectly flat and vertical.

11 To cut the tenon, shade the waste to clarify which portions should be cut away, then mount the tenon piece in the vice vertically and use a tenon saw to cut away the cheeks. Take care to cut on the waste side of the line, leaving the line intact (see JOINTS).

Alternatively tilt the wood and cut diagonally so two lines can be followed at the same time, giving greater saw control.

12 Using either the vice or a bench-hook, now saw the tenon cheeks across the grain exactly to the shoulder line. Accuracy is required as this shows on the finished joint.

Making a stub mortise using the mortiser

1 After preparing the wood to size, mark the position of the mortise on the wood. Select a chisel bit which corresponds to about one-third the thickness of the wood. Mark the depth of the mortise, which should extend to about two-thirds the width of the wood. Code the joints for clarity.

2 With a steel ruler calculate the position of the tenon dimensions and make two marks.

13 To remove the preparation marks, clean up both pieces with a very finely set plane. This is why the mortise width was marked at $\frac{1}{32}$ inch under the tenon width. Plane a slight bevel or "leading edge" on the end of the tenon. This will ease its path when it comes to assembling the joint.

14 Carefully drive the joint home using a hammer and scrapwood. If it is too tight, take the joint apart and examine where it is sticking and pare with a chisel; however, you should always aim for a joint "straight off the saw" rather than one you have to chisel back.

As the tenon was marked by $\frac{1}{32}$ inch oversize, carry out the final assembly of the joint in the vice. Plane the joint flush.

Using a radial-arm saw to cut a tenon

1 The tenon can be cut with a variety of power tools. Here the radial-arm saw is used to achieve the task swiftly. Set the blade height to the marks on the wood. (The guards have been removed for clarity of illustration.)

2 Clamp a stop to the saw table as a shoulder-line depth-stop. To remove the waste, hold the wood firmly against the fence, and pull the saw across in a series of cuts. Rotate the wood to cut the other shoulder.

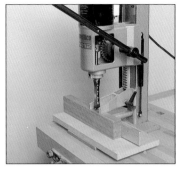

3 Set a marking gauge and line in the marks accurately, adjusting the gauge by knocking it on the bench (see MEASURING AND LAYING OUT) and gauge from both sides.

4 Set up the mortiser with the appropriate bit and set the depth guide, using the wood marks for alignment. Adjust the fence so that the bit aligns perfectly to the gauged lines, and position the top clamp so that the wood can slide comfortably underneath.

5 In a series of gentle cuts using the lever arm, chisel out the mortise, holding the wood firmly against the fence. Cut to the full depth in one pass.

6 Then slide the wood along so that the next cut overlaps the previous one. You may need to lift the bit clear for shavings to escape completely.

Fitting the joints

1 The finished mortise-and-tenon should have tight shoulder lines and be truly aligned as it is placed on the flat surface of the benchtop.

2 Now drive the joint together using a hammer and piece of scrapwood, and finally clean it up with a hand plane.

3 Now lower the saw to cut the tenon cheeks. Using the stop, pull the saw back in a series of cuts right up to the shoulder line. Take care on the final cuts as the shoulders must align all the way around the wood. Trim a slight bevel on the tip of the tenon.

PLANING

There is hardly any woodworking which does not include planing somewhere in its process, whether it is smoothing a surface flat, trimming joints true, or shaping a piece of wood to a given dimension. Any woodworking novice is likely to use a plane fairly early on, probably at the same time as they learn to use a saw.

The mastery of this age-old tool is highly satisfying, not least because of the sound and

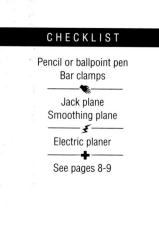

CHECKLIST

Pencil or ballpoint pen
Bar clamps
—————
Jack plane
Smoothing plane
—————
Electric planer
—————
See pages 8-9

smell of the wood shavings passing through the plane body.

Highly accurate planing can be achieved in a fraction of the time with an electric planer-thicknesser, but mastering the basics of hand planing first gives you more versatility and a better understanding of the character of wood.

Planes: shapes and sizes
Despite its simple function, the handplane has to be perfectly "in tune" to perform properly and therefore understanding its mechanics helps. There are several shapes and sizes of planes. The importance of size (length and weight) is best described by comparing the behavior of an oil tanker on a rough sea to a small tug. The longer plane will cut evenly through the undulations of a wavy board with sufficient weight to give it momentum, whereas a smaller plane will dip into the troughs and be thrown about.

For the beginner the best compromise is a plane which is heavy enough to avoid "chatter" (the blade not fully engaging with the wood fibers due to lightness), but not so long and heavy as to be cumbersome. A smoothing or small jack plane is therefore the ideal plane for the beginner. There are many makes of planes on the market, and they range from junk to masterpieces. It really is worth buying a good one even as a beginner.

Handplane mechanics
The plane blade is basically a wide chisel held in a finely adjusted jig (the plane body). The angle of the blade in the plane body is set (at 45 degrees), the adjusting knob controls the amount of blade protruding

Using a smoothing or jack plane

1 After sharpening the blade and setting it correctly (see TOOL MAINTENANCE), use a small practice piece of wood mounted in the vice to work out on.

2 Stand in line with the wood, leaning a little into the action (the direction of the cut), poised like a boxer with one foot in front of the other for stability.

through the mouth of the plane, and the lever checks that it is cutting parallel across the mouth and therefore not cutting grooves in the wood at one corner of the blade or the other. The plane blade is normally ground to about 25 degrees and its tip sharpened to about 35 degrees (see TOOL MAINTENANCE).

A cap iron is attached to the upper surface of the plane blade with its slightly hooked tip which is positioned ⅛ inch from the blade tip. This not only gives reinforcement to the blade tip, but causes the shaving to curl over and clear. Each time the blade is sharpened, the cap iron has to be removed, so its proper replacement is important!

A well set-up and razor-sharp plane is the vital prerequisite for successful planing. It is well worthwhile familiarizing yourself with all

the component parts of a plane and knowing their functions. Don't be frightened to take a plane to pieces and have a good look at it. You will learn more doing this yourself than any book can tell you.

A golden rule
There is one golden rule with planing (as with all sharp-edged tools) – the finer the cut, the less resistance of the material, and this results in greater control. The action of the handplane is simple. It is held in both hands, one hand to deliver the power and the other hand to apply pressure onto the wood to make sure that the blade bites.

The function of each hand overlaps as the plane travels across the wood, ensuring that contact is made at all times with the blade tip.

3 Mark lines across the wood with a pencil or ballpoint pen as "progress lines" and number equal intervals across the wood.

The idea is to plane off in one cut or "pass" all three lines at position 1 and work progressively across the work to position 7.

The lines indicate whether you are applying pressure consistently from the beginning of the cut to the end. The center of the plane should be lined up with each mark.

4 As the plane begins its journey, apply more pressure at the nose to keep the blade in perfect contact with the wood fibers. The plane body is in full contact with the wood, and the pressure between the hands is consistent hence maintaining blade tip contact at all times.

At the end of the stroke apply more pressure to the heel because the nose of the plane is now no longer in contact with the wood.

5 Constantly adjust and re-adjust the plane blade to give a controlled cut. If the cut is too thick, there will be less control of the plane. You may find you have to turn the wood around the other way to get a "silky" cut since the grain seldom runs perfectly parallel to the surface.

Use a straightedge to check the wood is flat at regular intervals so that planing and checking for trueness become one skill.

6 When planing, it is tempting to slice the plane at an angle. It is true that this will start the cut more easily, but there is a danger that you will plane the board out of true because the contact length of the plane's sole (or base) is reduced, and where there is reduced contact over a big area, accuracy is lost.

Planing wide boards

Wide boards can be planed diagonally or even across the grain to remove stock quickly and efficiently. This is because fibers are weak across the grain and therefore easily severed. A final smooth finish is achieved by planing with the grain.

Planing an edge "square" with a smoothing plane

Planing edges is a little more difficult. Planing an edge flat is straightforward, but getting it "square" (90 degrees) takes more practice.

If you find you are taking more off one side than the other, use your thumb to line up the center of the blade with the center of the wood. Use a try square to check that the wood is 90 degrees (see SQUARING WOOD).

Planing a chamfer (or angle)

1 Mark chamfers before planing them. An easy way to mark a chamfer is to use the thumb and fingers as a pencil gauge (see MEASURING AND LAYING OUT).

2 Make a series of light plane strokes with the plane held at the appropriate angle. Ideally the wood should be tilted so that the majority of planing is done horizontally. In this way the force of gravity on the plane helps with downward pressure. When holding the plane as shown, there is a risk of slippage, but with practice this is rarely a problem.

Planing wood using an electric planer-thicknesser

A planer-thicknesser can surface the side and edges of wood (on the top of the machine) and in this mode it is hand-fed by the operator, and it can also make the opposite sides and edges parallel and flat in the thicknesser (underneath). For this operation it is equipped with automatic feed. It is well worthwhile running a piece of wood back through the machine after it has been planed and thicknessed on both sides completely on automatic feed to eliminate any small ripples. It is in areas such as this that power tools score so heavily over hand methods.

1 First stand facing or astride the machine within easy reach of the start/stop switch, and set the feed table height to make a fine cut. Adjust the guard so that the wood can pass underneath it. This is a vital safety precaution as your fingers should never be exposed to the swiftly rotating cutter block.

Planing end grain with a smoothing plane

1 End grain will split if the fibers are not supported at the end of the plane stroke. The simplest method is to chisel or plane a small chamfer at the end of the wood, and this you can see just under the front knob of the plane. This ensures that the fibers slope away and are not touched by the plane blade, but they remain to give support to the rest of the wood.

2 On wide boards the end grain can be planed first from one direction, then the other. Take care to lift the plane at the end of the half-way stroke to avoid splitting the fibers on the other end. By using this method the end fibers are pushed against the rest of the wood rather than away from it. This then tends to compress them rather than split them out.

3 For shorter end grain work, a supporting block can be made, slightly wedge shaped to fit in the vice or a bar clamp. Take care to ensure the level of the waste piece is flush. If it is too high, it will obstruct the plane blade, and if it is too low, it will not support the fibers and they will still split out.

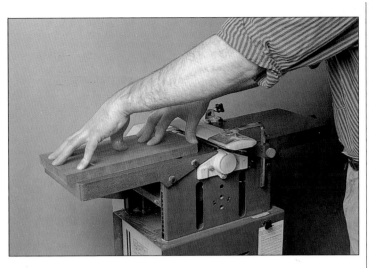

2 Switch on the machine and pass the wood over the cutter, holding the wood down at both ends with each hand. The fingers are always on top of the wood except for a minimal finger grip to pull the wood through.

3 As the wood is fed into the cutter, maintain firm downward pressure all the time. "Walk" the fingers across the guard to maintain the momentum. Some woodworkers prefer to use the palms of their hands for maximum friction grip and ease of operation as the hand passes over the guard. The important factor is safety and keeping fingers well away from the cutter.

4 The board is passed straight through to the end of the surfacing table. Your stance astride the machine gives equal reach for infeed and outfeed, especially on larger machines. On a smaller machine, such as the one shown here, and which home woodworkers are most likely to own, this is not necessary. Smaller boards require the use of a push stick (see JIGS AND JIGMAKING).

Edge planing with an electric planer

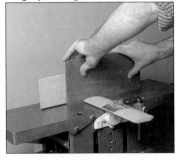

1 Set the fence in position and check it is "square" to the surfacing table. Position the guard so that it covers the bit up to the board.

Feed the wood against the fence. Taking care to avoid the unguarded portion of the cutter block, make a series of light cuts. Check with a square for accuracy and readjust the fence angle if necessary.

2 To plane an angled edge, set the adjustable fence to the desired angle, using a sliding bevel (see MEASURING AND LAYING OUT) and operate as for step 1. Ensure strict contact is made between the wood and the machine surfaces.

Using a thicknesser to make perfectly parallel cuts

1 Check the thickness of the wood and set the thicknessing table to the height of the cut (no more than approximately $1/16$ inch. Feed the wood into the thicknessing table. The automatic feed rollers will engage with the wood and plane the piece. On aluminum-cast machines, there is more natural friction between the metal and the wood, so use a little lubricant such as talcum powder to keep the wood moving.

2 Make a series of cuts to the desired dimension, turning the handle a few degrees for each pass. After a while you learn to judge how much to turn each time. The final finish is achieved by turning the wheel a mere fraction.

Using a jig

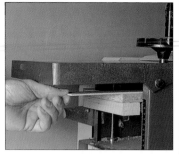

An MDF or melamine-faced board can be easily made up with an end batten screwed on to fix it in place. You can then feed very thin pieces of wood along the tip of the false platform using it as a support. In theory you can plane completely through the board into the platform – so take care to control the cut. Even with the planer blades correctly balanced and razor sharp, it is not advisable to cut down to a thickness of board less than ⅛ inch. With wild or interlocking grain, there is the risk of fibers breaking as the cutter engages against the grain.

Using the thicknesser to plane tapered or beveled pieces

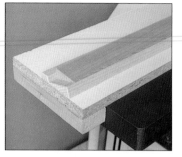

1 The false platform can be modified to support triangular-sectioned work by attaching longitudinally the appropriate shaped supporting strips.
The work is either rough-sawn first or fed into the thicknesser in rectangular form and reduced in a series of passes to the desired taper. The principle is that the cutter block can only make a parallel cut to the thicknessing table and therefore the wood must go to that shape.

2 The wood is lifted from the outfeed end of the thicknesser at the end of its journey. You should take care not to press the wood down as its release from the rear guide rollers as it comes past them can force the end of the wood back up into the cutter block and this will then cut off more than is required. It is interesting to note here that even when using power tools, as opposed to hand tools, some degree of skill is still involved.

Using a portable electric planer

This is a versatile tool for quick stock removal and finishing wood, and it has the advantage of being able to handle particularly long and heavy boards which would be cumbersome to feed through a planer-thicknesser. Instead the board is stationary, and the tool taken to it. Hold the planer firmly because when it is switched on its rotary cutter tends to pull it forward as it engages with the wood, and this action can be quite vigorous.

1 You will find it best to use both hands and "skate" the planer along the surface of the wood to maintain even flatness. The depth of cut is set by an adjusting knob which lowers or raises the front part of the planer's soleplate or base.

2 The portable planer is particularly useful for removing stock quickly across the grain. The fibers are weak in this direction and break up easily. Give the piece a final finish with the grain.

3 The portable planer can be turned over and set in a specially built table – again these are quite cheap to buy – and used as a mini-jointer. With its fence attached, you can "square" up wood quite easily.

ROUTING

The electric plunge router is almost unprecedented as a modern woodworking tool because of its enormous creative potential. It is probably the most creative tool in the workshop, limited only by your imagination.

It is basically an electric motor with a sharp-edged rotating bit at the end of its spindle, and its simplest function is in converting a hole into a groove by simply plunging the bit into the wood and pulling the tool via its adjustable fence across the wood, rather like a marking gauge. When you extend the range of bits to include profiled shapes of different size and variety, and then expand the function of the fence, which serves as a guiding jig by using other types of jigging device, the router does not stop at just cutting grooves and rabbets.

It can profile edges, cut through wood to any shape, cut joints, trim wood flat, make screw threads, and much more. Despite its simplicity of concept, the router is indeed a very sophisticated shaping tool. The three main elements of routing are: the size of the router, the variety of bits, and the types of jigging devices.

Router sizes

There are primarily three main sizes of router, specified by their collet (chuck/cutter shank) diameter and power rating: small ¼-inch collet routers are rated from about 400 watts to 750 watts (approximately 1 horsepower); ⅜-inch collet routers range from about 750 watts to 1,300 watts; and ½-inch collet routers range up to about 2,000 watts.

Bit size

Bits are available in ¼, ⅜ and ½-inch shank diameters. Collet sleeves allow smaller diameter cutters to be used in larger collet routers.

The range of bits is greater in the larger and stronger shank size, but it is deceptive to consider that routing creativity relies on numerous bits: a handful of basic profiles can be used for a variety of purposes.

Bits are made of high-speed steel (HSS) or tungsten-carbide-tipped steel (TCT). The latter are more expensive, but last many times longer.

CHECKLIST

Small, medium, or large router
with appropriate collet sleeves
Straight fence
Wheel fence
Guide bushings
Batten and "C" clamps
MDF template material
Double-sided tape
Selection of bits (straight, radiused,
rounding over, "V" groove, dovetail)
Router table
Drill stand with 1⅝ inches collar

— ✚ —

See pages 8-9

Jigging devices

The most basic jigging device is the adjustable straight fence which is attached to the router. It is used for straight grooves and rabbets parallel to the edge of the wood. The fence can also be used for cutting MORTISE-AND-TENONS. Other jigs include the roller guide which allows parallel cuts to be made on a concave or convex edge and a variety of guide bushings which are used against shaped templates.

BIT TYPES AND GUIDE BUSHING APPLICATION

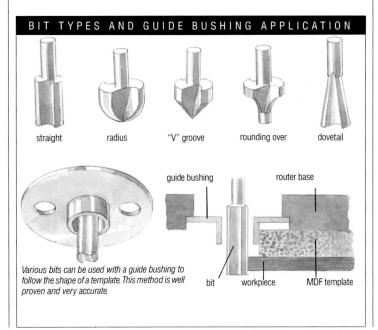

straight   radius   "V" groove   rounding over   dovetail

guide bushing   router base

bit   workpiece   MDF template

Various bits can be used with a guide bushing to follow the shape of a template. This method is well proven and very accurate.

Setting up

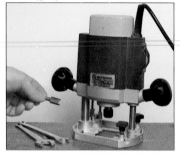

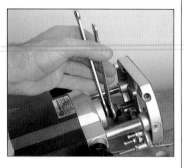

1 Bits are fragile and expensive. Most new bits are protected in an oiled plastic coating which you need to peel off. The plunge router usually requires two wrenches to tighten the collet chuck once the bit has been inserted, although increasingly routers have a spindle lock and just one wrench.

2 There is a knack to tightening and loosening the collet chuck when you use two wrenches. Wrap your hand around both wrenches and squeeze. When loosening, it is very easy to slip and graze your knuckles.

First steps in freehand routing

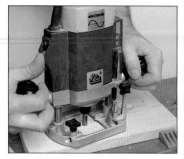

1 To get the "feel" of a router, try freehand routing shallow grooves (a simple name plaque is a good first exercise). First set the bit to depth using the depth-stop. A golden rule is to cut in depth no more than half the diameter of the bit in one pass (stroke).

2 It is important that the power switch is within finger reach. With the router switched off, position the bit where you want to plunge the first cut. Now switch on and firmly but slowly plunge into the wood to the depth-stop. As you do this, start the horizontal movement, passing the router freehand over the marked line. Keep the bit moving.

Template routing using a guide bushing

1 Creative routing can be achieved by using a guide bushing as a spacer between the bit and a template for grooving and edge trimming.

The guide bushing is a lipped collar which is screwed into the router base. There is a variety of diameter lips relating to different bit diameters. The general rule is to coordinate a measurement of ⅛ inch between bit edge and lip edge. Allow for this measurement when making the shaped template.

2 Use double-sided tape to fix the MDF template onto the slightly oversize wood. "C" clamps can be used, but they have to be moved around to allow the router to pass. A long straight bit is used here to finish a rough-sawn edge perfectly smooth and square. The guide bushing makes contact with the MDF template, and a series of cuts progressively works through to full depth. For such long bits a large capacity router is usually required.

Using a router head in the drill stand

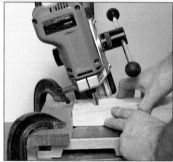

1 Simple drilling or milling (horizontal grooves) can be achieved with some routers with a standard 1⅝-inch collar. This router is released from its plunge/base assembly. It is inserted into matching 1⅝-inch collar of a drill stand and tightened.

2 The router can be used for drilling much cleaner holes than a normal twist-bit or flat-bit, but you have to be careful to avoid burning the wood as the debris has to escape.

This drill stand has a tilting head which makes the router even more versatile for special jigged operations, including doweling at an angle (see DOWEL JOINTS).

3 At the end of the stroke, release the plunge lock (either untwist the hand grip or use the plunge-locking lever) and the bit will spring back up. You can see that in this simple freehand exercise keeping to the line is not crucial, but it offers excellent practice in controlling the tool. Try to avoid burn marks.

Using the straight fence

The straight fence is supplied with the router as standard kit, and it can be adjusted to width to rout grooves, rabbets, and edge profiles such as chamfers (using a vee cutter). You will need to attach a wooden facing strip to the fence because for this and other operations a cutaway is required in the fence. It is common practice for woodworkers to make up their own wooden fences for routers and indeed for other tools such as circular saws.

To cut a simple chamfer, set the bit to depth, lock the plunge mechanism, and pull the router along the wood, keeping the fence in strict contact with the edge, just like a marking gauge (see MEASURING AND LAYING OUT).

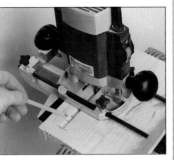

Two screws adjust the fence for cutting grooves. This stopped groove is simply marked first, and the groove is cut in steps by a series of "passes." You can see the three stages by which the groove is being executed. This maximizes the life of the bit and does not overload a small router. It is always good practice to take several small cuts rather than one large one.

Batten routing

By securing a straightedge onto the workpiece using "C" clamps, a versatile jig can be made. When calculating where to place the batten in relation to the desired cut, the crucial measurement is taken from the edge of the router base to the bit. Straight, vee-grooved, or radiused bits can be used to make different profiled cuts. Apply firm pressure toward the batten.

Using a router table

1 Most routers attach into a readymade table converting the tool into a mini-spindle molder. The position and height of the bit are fixed and the wood passed over the table surface against the appropriate jig. In this case a straight fence and straight bit are being used to form a rabbet. Press the wood firmly into the base/fence as it passes over the bit, keeping fingers well clear.

2 The router table is set up with a wheel guide for profiling convex and concave work. Here a radiused edge is being cut. The final finish is achieved with sandpaper (see ABRADING).

Cutting a tenon using the router

1 A straight fence and straight bit are used. Two marks are made on the wood to indicate the settings of the straight fence and the depth of bit.

To set the fence to the correct width, place the router with its bit lowered to just above the wood surface. Set the depth-stop to the vertical mark.

2 Work the router along the edge by first setting to half depth and cut back to the shoulder (up to the fence).

Set the depth-stop to full depth-of-cut and work the router across, taking great care to keep the router sole flat against the wood and not tilt it so the bit cuts below the intended path. Now reverse the wood and cut the other tenon cheek.

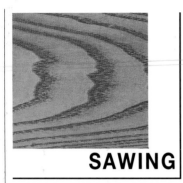

SAWING

You will probably find that sawing is your first task in woodworking. Before a piece of wood can be shaped or featured, it has to be cut from the board. Sawing is also an important technique throughout the making process – whether it be in conjunction with chiseling to cut joints, or roughing out tapers, curves, and other features, which are later finished smooth (see ABRADING, PLANING).

The saw is one of the oldest tools, and its action is very simple. A series of teeth are set outward in alternate directions along a flat steel blade and sharpened to a critical angle. This angle is determined by the type of work the saw has to do, and the manufacturers set them accordingly. The saw cuts a channel in the wood by severing the fibers rather like a row of miniature chisels. The groove the saw cuts is fractionally wider than the thickness of the saw in order to give clearance. This is called the "saw kerf." Because wood behaves differently along the grain from the way it does across the grain, there are saws for ripping and for crosscutting. These are differentiated by their number of teeth and pitch angle. There is a family of finer-toothed saws with thinner blades which are reinforced by a backing strip, and these are called "backsaws," of which the tenon saw is the most common. The technique of sawing accurately by hand has to be learned by practice. Like planing by hand, it depends for its success very largely on the quality and correct setting of the tool. Most woodworkers nowadays have saws set and sharpened by "saw doctors," mainly because it is not too expensive and it saves a lot of time. It is not however difficult to do it yourself with a little perseverance. Buying a quality saw in the first place will eliminate a lot of problems.

Saws for cutting curves include pad saws, coping saws, and bow saws, although these have now been largely superseded by powered saws such as jigsaws, scroll saws, and bandsaws.

Power saws
Everyone is familiar with the whine of a circular saw which can be heard beyond the walls of the woodworker's shop. Indeed the marriage of electric power with modern saw-blade technology has resulted in extremely accurate and smooth cutting saws, relying on harder-wearing tungsten carbide (TC) for the tips. These "tipped" saws are very much more expensive than ordinary steel ones, but they easily prove their worth in their cutting abilities and duration of service.

The radial-arm saw is a highly creative overhead circular saw with a universally angled saw head. It uses a standard circular saw blade, or for wider cuts for jointing it uses multi-cutters called dado cutters. These can cut wider grooves or trenches

Using a handsaw
The handsaw can be used for cutting wood of fairly thick dimensions either across or along the grain. When designed for cutting along the grain, they are known as rip saws, and for across the grain as crosscuts. They are however to some extent interchangeable. The rip saw has a wider "set" on the teeth because working down the grain of the wood makes it more difficult to clear away the waste. Crosscutting severs the fibers cleanly and is therefore less of a problem. You can support the wood by clamping it to the bench or supporting it lower on a saw horse or any firm base.

First draw a line across the wood (the line can be extended down the edge). This makes the cut easier to "sight up." You can use the thumb of your supporting hand to guide the path of the saw initially. Draw the saw gently back to start the motion of the first cut, guiding the flat side of the blade against your upturned thumb.

and are useful for making joints.

Perhaps the most efficient, and quietest, of saws is the bandsaw with its narrow continuous blade running around either two or three wheels, one of which is electrically driven. The flexible blade makes it suitable for cutting curves and straight lines. It also has a deceptive capacity for cutting thick boards. The convenient smaller versions of these electric saws are portable circular saws and jigsaws, either cord-operated or cordless.

Grip the handle firmly with the index finger pointing forward to give greater control over the stroke. You may need to use a knee to support the wood. Once the first and most difficult cut is made, use a steady motion to saw through the board. Jamming the saw in its groove can be avoided if you make sure your eye is directly in line with the saw blade.

SAW SPECIFICATION

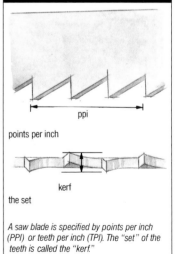

ppi

points per inch

kerf

the set

A saw blade is specified by points per inch (PPI) or teeth per inch (TPI). The "set" of the teeth is called the "kerf."

Using a backsaw

1 The backsaw, such as a tenon or dovetail saw, has a greater number of finer teeth than on a handsaw. Because of this, the backsaw gives a cleaner and more accurate cut. Secure the wood in a bench-hook mounted in the vice, positioning the marked line on the wood with the end of the bench-hook. The saw is drawn gently back across the wood against the end of the hook to make the first cut.

2 After the first cut has been made on the waste side of the line, gradually work the saw cut back along the surface of the wood, following the line to make a full-width saw channel. Then concentrate on sawing "square" to the vertical line by checking every ⅛-inch depth of cut. Your eye should be directly above and in line with the saw blade.

3 The greatest difficulty in using a tenon saw is in maintaining a "square" cut and not wandering off it. Therefore the first few cuts need to be closely monitored: stop, look, and correct the path of the saw if necessary. After a certain depth – approx ¼ inch – the saw cut itself will largely guide the subsequent path of the saw, so if it is not accurate, it will throw the saw off-course.

4 The backsaw can be used for cutting along and across the grain, and a vice is commonly used to support the wood. This frees your other hand, which can be used to give extra control. By using both hands, your elbows provide a stable pivoting system, you deliver more power and therefore more control, and your eye is naturally drawn in line with the blade, making it easier to follow the vertical line.

Using a coping saw

 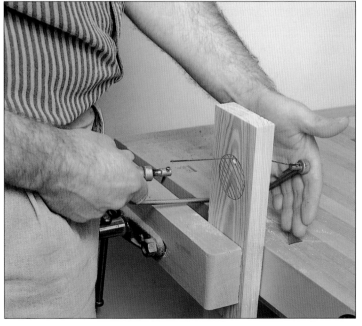

1 Whereas a tenon saw can only saw straight into the wood, the coping saw is useful for cutting curves or removing stock quickly. Hold the saw with both hands. Generally the teeth cut on the backward stroke, but you will find it works both ways. The blade can be rotated and set by twisting the handle so that the saw cuts in any desired path.

2 The coping saw can be used for cutting internal shapes such as large holes. First drill a hole on or near the line to take the saw blade. To insert the blade, push the frame against your hip, positioning the wood in the vice accordingly. Loosen the handle by unscrewing it and locate the blade bayonets in their seatings. Tighten up the handle with blade-holding pin extensions lining up to ensure that the blade is not twisted.

Using a power jigsaw

The electric jigsaw has a short reciprocating blade with teeth facing upward. It is a versatile tool for sawing straight and curved work, usually to a line. It is easy to operate once you learn to keep the pressure constantly against the surface of the wood to counteract the upward snatching of the blade. The jigsaw is capable of removing stock in tight areas such as curves and narrow slits (the bandsaw has a similar capacity).

Using a portable circular saw

1 Circular saws are used for straight cuts across or along the grain and can be set to full or part depth by lowering or raising the blade. The blade can also be adjusted to cut at an angle. You can use the saw to cut "freehand" along a marked line by positioning the tool at the appropriate mark. Use both hands firmly on the handles to control the saw, and start the motor before the blade engages with the wood.

2 The standard straight fence can be adjusted to make parallel cuts similar to a router (see ROUTING).

3 A clamped batten can serve as a guide for making straight cuts through the wood at any desired position or angle.

Using a bandsaw

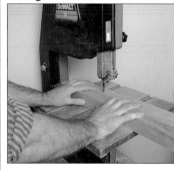

1 A bandsaw is a quiet, efficient machine for cutting both straight and curved work. Its continuous loop blade passes over two large diameter wheels. The "throat" of the bandsaw refers to the distance of the blade to the nearest part of the machine when measured across the table. This determines the length of the piece it can cut across the grain. The wood is supported on the saw's table.

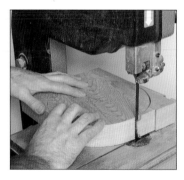

2 Being truly versatile, the bandsaw can cut circles or other curves to a marked line. Make sure your fingers are always away from the blade when supporting and feeding the work. Here the upper blade guide assembly is higher to show the line on the wood and is normally positioned about 1 inch above the wood.

3 The bandsaw is capable of cutting thick pieces of wood. This however should be done slowly, because a bandsaw blade is relatively fragile and also because the waste or sawdust in the cut needs time to clear to avoid overheating. The straight fence on the bandsaw can be used for repeat parallel cuts or for jigging square pieces (see JIGS AND JIGMAKING).

Using a radial-arm saw

1 The radial-arm saw is an overhead circular saw; the wood is mounted stationary on the table and the saw drawn across it. It is primarily used for crosscutting but also for rip, miter, and compound cuts. It has a facility for raising or lowering the saw for grooves and rabbets. The wood is held against the fence and lined up to the saw blade at the marked position for the cut.

Using a table saw

1 A table saw is used for straight cuts along and across the grain. You can raise, lower, and tilt the blade.

The sliding miter fence is set to 90 degrees for cutting wood across the grain. You should use both hands to grip the wood against and operate the sliding fence. The clamped block on the rip fence is used for repeat cuts. *Safety guard has been lifted for clarity of illustration.*

2 The table saw is used for single or repeat cuts along the grain (ripping), and the rip fence is first adjusted and tightened to position before the power is switched on. The riving knife is there to prevent the wood from closing in and jamming the saw cut as the wood passes through.

Use push sticks (easily cut on a bandsaw) to guide the wood along and against the fence.

3 The blade can be tilted to cut wood to any angle up to 45 degrees. The sliding fence is used and if set to 45 degrees will facilitate compound miter cuts.

4 The circular saw blade can be lowered to cut grooves using the rip fence as a guide. Grooves can be widened by adjusting the fence after each cut, and this is particularly useful for cutting the cheeks of tenons. Sometimes a jig is used to secure the wood as it is passed over the blade. Grooved or rabbeted cuts can be achieved by using the miter fence with the wood lying the other way.

2 The saw can be positioned at any angle to make a cut in the crosscut or fixed-head mode by simple adjusting knobs.

3 The rise and fall facility of a radial-arm saw opens up some unique creative possibilities beyond just cutting grooves or rabbets. Here a simple "V" cut jig (see JIGS AND JIGMAKING) secures a circular bowl blank (see TURNING WOOD) as the saw is drawn over it to skim the surface perfectly flat.

4 The radial-arm saw can be used for ripping boards down their length. Swing the saw around and lock it to the arm, then slightly lower the arm assembly as the blade spins to ensure the blade is fractionally lower than the table surface. The particle board or MDF saw table is an advantage for jigging, especially when lined with a pinned facing sheet of thin MDF which can take the saw cuts.

5 When ripping, it is important to feed the wood in against the rotation of the blades and to first set up the anti-kickback device which prevents the blade from grabbing the wood. *(Guards have been removed for clarity of illustration.)*

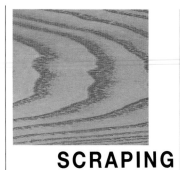

SCRAPING

The use of scrapers goes back at least as far as Neanderthal man. It is a primitive method of fashioning material and in particular wood. The action of a scraper is similar to that of a chisel, producing an extremely fine silk-like shaving. Because of this the scraper can be controlled to finish a surface delicately, especially where there is wild and irregular grain which might tear under a plane.

Scrapers produce a superior finish compared to sandpaper, which can clog the grain especially when very fine grits are used. Any sharp-edged sheet material will serve as a scraper, even a piece of glass. Cabinet scrapers are quality steel and usually straight-edged, although there are different profiles for curved work.

The scraper is used particularly for finishing veneered work and – because of its ability to remove very fine slivers at a time – for removing excess glue. As a finishing tool it can be slow but its distinctive sound, like that of a spokeshave, expresses the true spirit of woodworking.

Using a scraper

2 The amount of flex and angle of contact with the wood can influence the behavior of the scraper, so you might find it useful to experiment a bit.

1 Hold the scraper in both hands, wrapping the index fingers over the top edge slightly and pressing with the thumbs behind to flex the blade, so that it curves away from you.

3 For localized scraping, such as for trimming flush the inlay banding on this veneered panel, the tool is bent more severely.

4 Try and work with the grain or diagonally and avoid abrupt strokes across the grain which could tear the fibers.

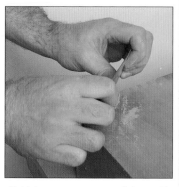

5 Using a scraper on solid wood is a traditional method of final finishing. For the best results sharpen the scraper frequently (see TOOL MAINTENANCE).

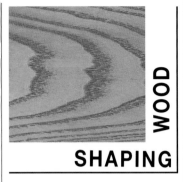

SHAPING WOOD

Often the tree itself is naturally shaped and curved, and yet when the board is sawn and planed it becomes straight. This imposition of man's will over nature is arguably a long cry from the nature of the tree, but for economic reasons the straight cut is advantageous.

Much furniture today is, however, "flat panel" work made from composite board such as particle board or MDF

CHECKLIST

Sanding sticks
"C" clamps
Compasses
Steel ruler
Sliding bevel
Paper
Scissors
Glue

Flat and convex spokeshaves
Carving gouge
Bevel-edged chisel
Blockplane or smoothing plane

Coping saw, jigsaw, or bandsaw

See pages 8-9

with curves "introduced," minimizing the waste of this valuable resource.

It takes time, often several hundred years, for the shapes and curves of a tree to form, and so too it takes time to produce curves in the process of working wood. Shapes and curves add great interest to a piece of furniture, and history is full of examples of the extravagant and skillful shaping of wood. The styles vary greatly from individuals such as the 18th-century British woodcarver Grinling Gibbons to the present-day designer John Makepeace.

Curved and shaped work is also characteristic of specific craft traditions such as boatbuilding and musical-instrument making. Indeed entire cultures express the bendiness of the natural tree in their furniture traditions such as the Scandinavian tradition of wood laminating and steam bending (see BENDING WOOD).

Wood can also be shaped or curved by coopering, bricking, stack laminating, saw kerfing, or simply cutting to shape from solid wood. The age-old practice of searching for the right piece of wood which presents the natural structural curve is still in our consciousness despite the evolution of shaping techniques, especially those whereby the curve is imposed on the grain of the wood.

Imposing curves or shapes onto the grain

Most curves in woodwork are imposed onto the grain as opposed to following it, but you still have to observe the nature of the grain to obtain adequate strength. Here the piece will be weak at the top where the grain is very short.

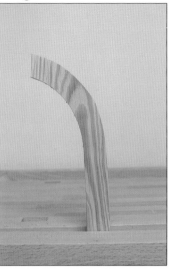

In this hoop with the grain running vertically, the checks indicate adequate grain strength and the crosses indicate weak or "short" grain. When introducing curves in a piece of woodwork, try to avoid short grain as the wood is likely to break along it.

A simple and economical way to introduce a curve at the end of a straight piece is to glue on an extra piece ensuring the grain matches. In the step above, the shaded portion and cutaway section show the intended shape.

Shaping with a spokeshave

1 Imposed curves can be easily laid out (see MEASURING AND LAYING OUT) and cut with a variety of saws (see SAWING). Finish with a flat-bottomed spokeshave, working in the direction of the arrows to cut with the grain and holding the spokeshave between fingers and thumbs. Rotate the wood in the vice to make sure you are always cutting more or less horizontally.

2 A convex-bottomed spokeshave can be used to cut concave shapes. You can also achieve a fine finish by abrading (see ABRADING). Note the arrows indicate the change of cutting direction to go with the grain.

Shaping three dimensionally from a solid piece of wood

1 This curved stool or table leg can be easily sawn to a rough shape, having first marked the lines on two adjacent surfaces. The bandsaw is ideal for this task.

2 Hold the leg in a vice or clamp it to the bench (see CLAMPING AND HOLDING), then shape with a spokeshave or carving gouge. Hold the gouge like a chisel (see CHISELING) and pare away the fibers working with the grain. Always keep the gouge razor sharp (see TOOL MAINTENANCE).

Brick and stack laminated constructions

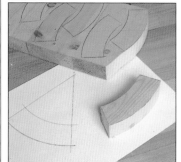

1 Brick construction has numerous applications. Traditionally it is used to create curves for bowed drawer fronts which are veneered afterward (see VENEERING). The technique involves laying out the required curved segment, then tracing or transferring the data onto a piece of wood which acts as a template for marking all the bricked pieces.

2 The pieces can be cut on the bandsaw and then glued together using a rubbed joint or by clamping if you feel this is necessary. The more accurate you are in sawing to the line, the less trimming you will need to do afterward to finish the curve evenly.

3 Stack laminating involves the vertical gluing of any identically shaped pieces of wood. It can include plywood, in which case the ply is also a decorative feature.

Making a coopered shape

1 Coopered work involves the segmenting of identical pieces to form a part or whole circle. First mark the segments by scribing two concentric circles, dividing them into the required number of segments and converting the curved sides into two flat sides. With a steel ruler and sliding bevel, the relevant data is transferred to a length of wood.

2 The wood is then planed (see PLANING) and sawn (see SAWING). The angles are obviously critical in the laying out and cutting. Glue the segments together (see GLUING). A rubbed joint should suffice; i.e., it is not necessary to clamp them. Leave the segments to dry on a flat papered surface to prevent the assembly from sticking to the bench.

3 When the joints are dry, mark a line and you can then trim the outer edge by a variety of means. Here a chisel is used with the grain, but you can also sand the curve (see ABRADING).

4 Alternatively a plane can be used. In this method the end grain is showing so you will be planing across the grain and hence the fibers will cut willingly. For ease of working rotate the wood in the vice, keeping the plane more or less horizontal.

5 The inner curve can be finished by sanding or using a firmer gouge. You will find that a good way to finish the inside is to wrap some coarse sandpaper around a shaped stick and work horizontally.

Twisting wood to form shapes

Twisting wood is a novel way of shaping; experiment using thin solid wood or plywood. Here a few layers of thin plywood have been clamped and turned to demonstrate the simplicity of the method. A simple jig can be improvised to hold the clamps in the desired position (a length of wood in the vice can be clamped to the upper clamp). The twist maintains adequate pressure if a fairly liberal coating of plastic resin glue is used. Such decorative twists can be veneered either before or after to give the appearance of a solid piece. Clean up the edge using a spokeshave or sanding stick.

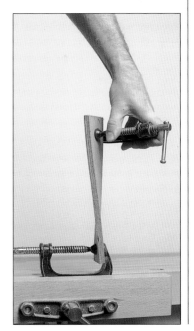

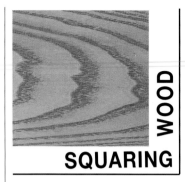

WOOD

SQUARING

Woodworking depends on accuracy – which usually means working to a line – it is important to make sure the wood is accurately cut to size beforehand. This technique is called "preparation of wood" or "squaring."

When wood has been bought rough-sawn or even pre-planed it requires squaring, not least of all because there are likely to be twists or bows, especially in softwoods which are not fully seasoned.

A piece of wood has been squared when all surfaces are flat, adjacent surfaces are 90° to each other and opposite surfaces are parallel. You may find it necessary, when making a table, for instance, to prepare accurately four identical pieces for the legs and a series of identical pieces to edge-joint the top together (see cutting lists in DRAWING). Hence the need for a standard squaring procedure.

The full procedure is achieved by either hand or power tools, the latter being far quicker. You will find it is an advantage to practice the hand process first, however painstaking, as such difficulty leads to a full appreciation of the need for skill and accuracy.

Squaring wood by hand

1 Select the best side (face side) and plane it flat and smooth (see PLANING). Hold the work on the benchtop using dogs or stops, checking with a straightedge or ruler. Now mark the first side with a face side mark which extends to the best edge (face edge). Face marks are important when gauging or using a square, the stock is normally placed against the face side or face edge.

2 Mount the wood low in the vice and plane the face edge square (90 degrees) to the face side. Check the accuracy with a try square and steel ruler.

Mark the face edge mark so it adjoins the face side mark.

3 A marking gauge is set to gauge to width. Use it vertically with the spur touching the appropriate calibration on the steel ruler.

Now mount the wood at an angle in the vice and carefully gauge to width, trailing the spur at a shallow angle and ensuring the stock is kept firmly against the face edge. Mark a line all the way around the wood.

CHECKLIST

Steel ruler
Marking knife
Pencil or ballpoint pen
Marking gauge
Try square
Tenon or dovetail saw

Smoothing or jack plane

Planer-thicknesser
Table saw or
Radial-arm saw or
Bandsaw or
Jigsaw

See pages 8-9

8 Shade in the waste with a pencil or ballpoint pen ready for cutting the ends off.

Using a bench-hook mounted in the vice, saw off the ends with a tenon saw on the waste side of the line.

9 Finally, if necessary, trim the end grain with a plane. Take care to avoid splitting the end grain by using a supporting block in the vice.

4 Shade the waste portion and then mount the wood in the vice and plane to width. As you approach the line, adjust the plane to cut a fine shaving.

Almost as the marking gauge line is reached, a fine sliver of wood can be easily rubbed away at each edge, indicating that only a few fine plane strokes are required to reach the line. In theory the edge should be perfectly square.

5 Check the minimum thickness of the wood and set the marking gauge, this time to gauge the thickness. Now gauge to thickness a line all the way around the wood. With a little practice you can quickly gauge holding the wood freehand. Plane to thickness, taking care to check constantly the line after a few plane strokes.

6 Square to length using a try square, steel ruler, and marking knife. First set the zero of the steel ruler against one end of the wood and measure in about ¼-inch. This is the minimum amount of wood which can be easily cut off with a tenon saw. Now move the steel ruler so that the zero lines up with the ¼-inch mark and measure the required length (leaving at least ¼ inch).

7 You should use the try square with its stock against the face edge. Locate the marking knife in the first mark, slide the try square up to it, and mark a line carefully across. Locating the knife in the previous cut line, square the line all the way around the wood, keeping the stock of the try square against either face side or face edge. This is important to ensure that the lines meet up.

Squaring wood by machine

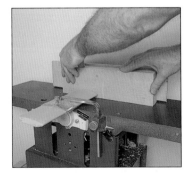

1 First cut the wood slightly oversize as straight as possible (length + 1 inch width + ¼ inch thickness + ⅛ inch.)

Using a planer-thicknesser, surface plane the face side, making a few passes until it is flat (see PLANING). Make sure the guard is in place, and pass your hands over it as you push the wood through. Pencil a face side mark on the planed side.

2 Now set the fence at 90 degrees and plane the face edge square and true. Pencil a face edge mark onto the edge.

3 Set the thicknessing table to the width of the piece of wood and feed in the piece. A few passes will be required, adjusting the cut with the hand wheel.

4 Finally, set the thicknessing table to the thickness of the wood and feed in the wood to reduce in stages to the desired dimension. If the board is wide, use a steel ruler and marking knife, ballpoint pen, or pencil to mark a parallel line. Shade in the waste and plane down to the line. Measure the precise length required and mark with a pencil, then saw off using a table saw, radial-arm saw, etc.

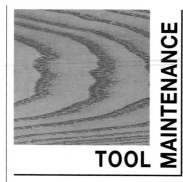

TOOL MAINTENANCE

All woodworking tools need maintaining, even if it is only a light coating of oil to prevent a steel blade from rusting. Many woodworking tools have a sharp cutting edge and, apart from files and "hard-tipped" saws (which are discarded when blunt), these edges need truing up, setting, honing, or – in some cases – grinding, to restore them to optimum working order.

The importance of a razor-sharp edge for a marking knife, a plane blade, or chisel can only be emphasized by describing the effects of using blunt tools.

Blunt tools are virtually useless and lead to disastrous results: a blunt marking knife tears rather than incises the grain, a blunt chisel fails to cut. The beginner may also not realize that the cutting angle of the chisel greatly affects its performance irrespective of the sharpness of its tip.

The importance of regular maintenance

Increasingly, hand- and powered saws have hard-tipped blades which offer many times the life of re-sharpenable blades, but which are thrown away when dulled. It is not always apparent when the cutting edge is dull. Only comparison with a replacement blade/tool makes it obvious.

To get the most out of your tools, you should maintain them regularly. A chisel blade dulls every time it is worked into the grain. It takes seconds to "touch up" or hone the blade on an oilstone. Many new tools are supplied either blunt or crudely sharpened so the ritual of grinding and honing should begin as soon as the tool is taken from its box.

Router bits (see ROUTING) need proper care and servicing as they are expensive, brittle, and prone to resin clogging, which leads to heat build-up and fast blunting because of the high speed of revolution. Woodworking is about care, attention, and pride, and this starts with your own tools.

Dismantling and grinding a plane blade

The modern steel smoothing or jack plane is a precision instrument and requires proper setting up each time the blade is taken out for sharpening. This should be done frequently, as a plane can never be sharp enough and dulls each time it engages with the wood. If a handplane is suddenly jolted or dropped against the benchtop, the blade can be knocked out of true. A handplane needs constant attention, adjusting, and – above all – must be kept razor-sharp. To dismantle the plane, lift the lever on the lever cap and lift out the blade assembly.

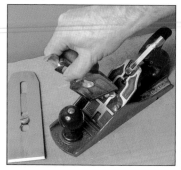

1 The cap can be used as a screwdriver for tightening the blade-assembly screw for the correct cap lever pressure. Use the cap to unscrew the cap-iron screw and then take the blade apart ready for grinding or sharpening.

BLADE ANGLES

Chisels are bought from the manufacturer already ground at an angle of 25 degrees, and then they are honed further to an angle of 30 to 35 degrees, using an oilstone.

Simply place the chisel's beveled edge on the stone, raise the chisel handle very slightly to obtain the additional angle, and work the chisel back and forth until a fine new bevel is formed. Follow the same procedure for a plane blade.

25° 30°

5 Now the plane blade is "backed off" to remove the burr which the sharpening has caused. Repeat the sharpening and backing off process. Finally the fine burr is removed with a leather strop or by simply cutting into the edge of a piece of wood.

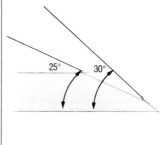

2 Normally the plane blade requires only occasional grinding, if a nick has been taken off the edge. Here the electric bench grinder is used. Feed the blade against the wheel at an angle of about 35 degrees. Move the blade sideways across the wheel using the fingers to maintain pressure at a fixed angle.

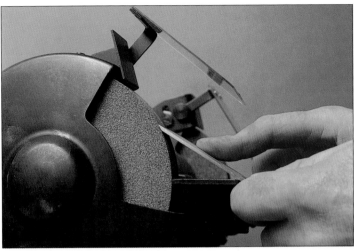

3 It takes some practice to grind a blade neatly. The important thing to do is maintain a consistent angle. To help, you can mark the blade where the tool rest makes contact. Never grind bevels or curves on the plane blade. The blade should be perfectly straight across.

4 It is important to sharpen just one side of the blade (the ground-angled side) and to leave the other side absolutely flat. Hold the plane blade firmly with both hands. The motion and the spread of the fingers and locking of the wrists helps maintain the angle (about 25 degrees). Work the blade into the oilstone or diamond stone in a series of definite back-and-forth strokes.

6 The cap iron is screwed back onto the plane blade, leaving a gap of about ¹/₁₂ inch at the tip. This is crucial for forming the shaving, and perfect contact should exist between these two pieces of metal to avoid shavings getting trapped between them.

7 When you have inserted the blade assembly back into its housing, the final adjustments are made with the screw adjuster and tilting lever. Turn the plane upside-down and look down the sole, using screw and lever to adjust the blade so it protrudes fractionally giving a parallel shadow.

Sharpening a chisel

1 Chisels need frequent sharpening just like plane blades. Grip the chisel with both hands and work the blade in the same way as for sharpening a plane blade. The locking of the wrists helps prevent a curved edge from forming.

2 Sharpening the chisel blade at a slightly shallower angle increases its cutting efficiency, though in theory it makes the tip more brittle.

Sharpening a scraper

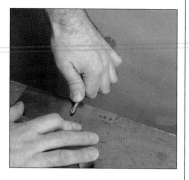

1 Any oblong piece of quality steel can be used as a scraper. Its cutting action relies on a burr which is formed by first draw-filing the edge flat. Use both hands on the file and work it up and down the scraper edge. The scraper is first mounted low in a vice.

2 Now use a slipstone or diamond stone to hone the edge of the blade. A burr is created by stroking the scraper with a burnisher a few times with the blade down against the benchtop. Now the burr is turned by stroking each edge of the blade at a slight angle with the burnisher.

Grinding and sharpening a marking knife

1 A cordless grinder can be extremely useful around the workshop for grinding tools such as the marking knife. Here both edges are fed into the wheel with the rotation against the blade so that the burr is removed.

2 The marking knife should be constantly sharpened on an oilstone, using a light oil for lubrication.

Care of planer blades

Planer blades are usually throwaway TCT or re-sharpenable high-grade steel. It is not advisable to re-grind planer blades. They should be sent away for servicing, but minimal honing can be done to extend their life. It should be remembered that planer blades are balanced and that means they are identical in profile.

1 To remove or reset the planer blades, first use a wrench to release the blades from the clamps.

2 It is essential that both blades are set identically in their seatings, and this can be checked with two battens with marks aligning the outfeed table and the tip of the blades. The blades should just "kiss" the wood on both battens. Adjustments to raise the blades can be made with the Allen key and spring-loaded grub screws.

Lubricating planer tables

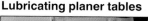

Most home workshop or light-industrial planer-thicknessers have aluminum beds which mean they tend to stick occasionally. At times a lubricant such as talcum powder can be applied to the thicknessing table surface to facilitate the automatic feed of the wood.

Care of routers and router bits

1 Router bits are expensive and fragile. Apart from careful storage in a box, they require regular maintenance, not least of all removal of wood resin from the cutting edge.

Using a diamond stone (for TCT cutters), carefully hone the inside edges. Do not hone the outside edges as the precisely balanced cutting action will be disturbed.

2 This tool creates dust, and it is the dust which can be a menace to its proper efficiency. Use a light oil to lubricate the plunge mechanism.

Grinding flat-bits

With care flat-bits can be "touched up" on the grinder, but excessive grinding will upset the balance of the identical cutters.

Grinding gouges

Gouges for turnery and carving are easily ground by rotating them slowly at a fixed angle against the toolpost of the grinder. Use the fingers as a seating for the rotating action.

Care of saws

Many saws nowadays are disposable with hard-tipped blades which cannot be re-sharpened. However, it is an advantage to be able to service your own saws and keep the edge constantly sharp.

1 First mount the saw between two straight pieces of wood in a vice and use a file to "top" the teeth level. Sometimes a file-holding jig is used, but you can acquire the knack by holding the file in the index finger and thumb of each hand and using the other fingers as a guide against the face of the saw to set up a firm filing motion.

2 The saw blade is now "set" with a special tool which bends each alternate tooth to a specific angle (adjusted on the tool according to the points per inch).

3 The final stage is to use a triangular section file to file each tooth so that it is sharp. Get into the motion of filing the alternate teeth and then repeat the action from the other side on the other teeth. A little candle wax applied to the saw blade helps with the action.

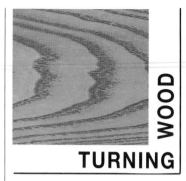

WOOD TURNING

Turning is one of the simplest techniques in woodworking, and it has enormous universal appeal. People are fascinated by watching wood being shaped on a lathe because the effect is immediate and the shapes alter so quickly. It is possibly one of the easiest techniques to learn, though to master it well there is no short cut to experience.

Anyone can learn how to use a lathe, a quiet, relatively inexpensive power tool which takes up little room, needing only a bench for mounting.

On the lathe you can turn small functional objects such as bowls, platters, goblets, and decorative items, as well as make turned components for furniture such as chair and table legs.

The principle of lathework is simply that the wood is rotated at speed in a holding device such as a chuck, and these come in various shapes and sizes to suit the type of work being undertaken.

A variety of differently profiled scrapers or gouges are carefully fed into the rotating wood against the firm support of a tool rest which acts as a stationary lever. These chisels or gouges are hand-held and moved by the operator to cut

various shapes. The final finish can be achieved on the lathe, either straight from the tool, by sanding (see ABRADING), by burnishing with shavings, or by applying wax as the work rotates. These techniques are explained in the following demonstrations. As lathework creates dust and chips which fly everywhere, protect your eyes and lungs with an appropriate mask/face shield.

Most woods lend themselves to turning. Some, such as pine, yew and elm are especially suitable. Elm is often turned "wet" – that is, as unseasoned wood still containing a high degree of sap.

Turning can make use of cutoffs which otherwise might be too small to use. Turning wood is a mesmerizing activity and once taken up will give endless hours of satisfaction.

CHECKLIST

Woodturning lathe or lathe attachment and power drill
Set of scrapers
Set of gouges
Sandpaper
Calipers
Tenon saw
Hot-melt glue gun
Screws
Drill and screwdriver

See pages 8-9

Faceplate turning: turning a bowl

1 Cut a bowl blank either octagonal or circular (see SAWING) and attach it to the faceplate by drilling pilot holes and screwing in place.

2 Mount the faceplate on the threaded drive spindle and rotate it by hand, aligning the tool rest and tool post so that they do not interfere, i.e., so the wood can rotate without touching any part of the lathe. Now set the tool post for height – in line with the center of the wood.

Faceplate work with a scraper

Although a gouge tends to be used by professionals, a scraper is also effective. Indeed it is easier to use although less efficient as a cutting tool. There is a wide variety of scraper profiles. Here the lip of the bowl is scraped flat. The tool rest is lowered so that the top of the scraper is in line with the center.

Checking the depth of a bowl

A simple method for checking the depth, and hence avoiding cutting through into the screws which hold the bowl to the faceplate, is to use a straightedge with the tool squeezed against it. Then transfer the screws to the edge where the thickness of the bowl blank can be judged. This is why short screws are used on bowl blanks – lots of them for maximum anchorage.

Using a gouge for faceplate turning

1 The gouge is the most efficient tool for cutting wood on the lathe. Hold it firmly with both hands, tilting the gouge at an angle so that the tip engages with the wood. Switch the lathe on and feed the gouge gently into the wood, resting the bevel of the tip on the wood first, then lifting the handle to engage the tip with the wood.

2 The profile of the outer edge of the bowl can be cut using the gouge. The lathe speed can be raised from slow to medium as the bowl becomes perfectly circular and hence balanced. Make sure the gouge is kept razor sharp by frequent grinding (see TOOL MAINTENANCE).

3 Now move the tool rest around to turn the face of the bowl. The height of the tool rest should be adjusted so that when the gouge is tilted, the tip is in line with the center. Begin gouging out the inside of the bowl, feeding the horizontal edge of the gouge tip forward.

4 The action usually starts at the center and works outward. A finer finish can be achieved after the roughing-out has been completed. As you remove more stock, you can move the tool rest closer, but only when the power is switched off do you make adjustments to the tool post; always take care to do this, a lathe can be very dangerous.

Finishing

1 Work through the grits from medium-coarse to medium, holding the sandpaper between the fingers and applying it against the rotation and slightly below the center. If the bowl is large, refrain from using the highest lathe speed. This should be reserved for spindle work, because it's safer.

2 Both hands can be used. If you press too hard, you will soon know because the sandpaper will get hot. Keep the sandpaper moving to avoid the grit forming "channels." It is advisable to link up some form of dust extraction system when sanding, as the dust is thrown centrifugally and can be dangerous if inhaled.

3 A handful of shavings can be fed against the rotating bowl. Some woods are more resinous than others and thus create a fine luster to the wood.

4 A wax can be applied while the work is spinning, but for lacquers or oils it is best to rotate the wood by hand. This is because lacquers and oils are much thinner than wax and would tend to splash. Here olive oil is being applied to the bowl, highlighting the grain.

Turning between centers: spindle turning

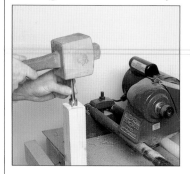

1 This method is applied to spindle turning. Sometimes spindle work can be very small such as for bobbins.

First prepare the wood either octagonal or square in section, cut two "V" grooves on one end, diagonally opposed, to find the center of the wood, and drive in the spur center with a mallet.

2 Mount the work on the lathe with the tapered end of the spur center slipping into the hollow mandrel. This center is called the drive center.

3 Move up the tailstock and tighten and then screw in the end center into the wood, first marking diagonals to locate the center. A live center rotates with the wood. A dead center relies on friction and needs tightening frequently as it wears when turned. A little wax can be used on the dead center to prevent friction burning.

4 Now set the tool post to position and adjust the tool rest for height and parallel alignment. Rotate the wood manually to check that it clears, i.e., it doesn't touch the tool rest.

Scraping hollows

An appropriately profiled scraper is used to cut hollows.

Feed the scraper in gently. Frequent grinding keeps the tool cutting efficiently (see TOOL MAINTENANCE).

Scraping convex "beads"

To shape convex "beads," use a flat scraper or chisel, sliding it in a horizontal arc against the tool post to form the curve.

Cutting slots and "parting"

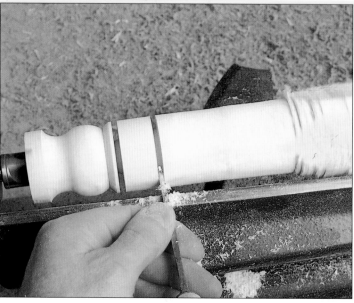

Either a parting tool or a narrow chisel can be used. The tool is driven into the rotating work, either for slotted features for decoration or for partially cutting off last of all.

Spindle work with a gouge

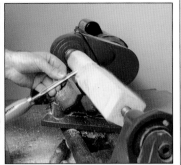

Tilt the gouge at an angle holding the handle firmly with one hand and rocking the gouge through the fingers and thumb of the guiding hand. Fast stock removal comes with practice as one edge of the gouge drives horizontally across the work.

Using a scraper for spindle work

1 After setting the tool rest so that the top of the scraper is in line with the center of the wood when held horizontally, feed the scraper gently into the revolving wood. The speed can be stepped up as the work becomes circular and properly balanced.

2 A wide chisel can be used as a scraper as it becomes a self-guiding jig for flat cuts.

Using calipers

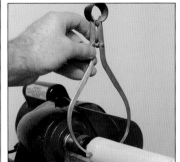

Calipers are used to check the diameter of the work, first setting them with the aid of a steel ruler. The work should be stationary when using calipers.

The hot-melt glue gun attachment method

This novel method used by the author offers a quick and easy way of turning small work, such as goblets and eggcups, on a wood-lined faceplate. Care should be taken when turning near the glue bond to avoid excessive heat build up.

First draw a series of concentric circles on the faceplate blank to center the wood.

1 Use a hot-melt glue gun to attach the wood to the faceplate. The wood has to be perfectly dry and flat at the end. When starting to turn, the tailstock can be used for extra support. The advantage of the method is in turning the end and tool access. Of course there are a number of chucks which achieve the same result as this improvised method.

2 After the end has been fashioned, you can then turn the sides to a slender profile. Notice the parting cut which will be done last of all – after sanding.

3 The turned object is sawn off with a tenon saw when the lathe is switched off. With experience you can completely part small objects on the lathe, and they will simply fall into your hand as they are released.

VENEERING

Veneering is one of the oldest woodworking techniques, dating back to before the Egyptians. It is also one of the most relevant techniques of modern times as it is an extremely efficient way of utilizing wood. A veneer is a wafer-thin piece of the tree; in fact, modern veneers measure about $1/50$ inch in thickness. That is the equivalent of a piece of heavy paper.

Veneer is glued onto a ground such as particle board or MDF, typically a table top. If a table top $1\frac{1}{8}$ inch thick is made of solid wood, it is easy to calculate just how many veneered table tops could be made from the same piece of wood, even allowing for wastage in cutting.

Veneered work is often associated with cheap furniture – and indeed much mass-produced veneered furniture does not last, but then the same can be said of much mass-produced solid wood furniture.

Throughout the history of furniture-making veneering has been used to demonstrate the sheer beauty of wood, and many fine examples of craftsmanship exist. But veneer has also been used to disguise shoddy workmanship and cheap constructions.

The advantage of veneer is that it gives the cabinetmaker a great deal more wood species to choose from. By restricting some rare species of wood for veneer cutting only, it has conserved those species or at lease extended their life.

Modern veneered work also overcomes many of the problems of wood movement associated with solid wood constructions, although early veneering was laid onto solid pine with inferior glues, leading to splitting and peeling. Today, particle board and MDF are excellent bases for veneered work because of their stability, and this coupled with superior glues such as white or yellow make it a technique which is appropriate in terms of conservation as well as being useful, reliable, and relatively inexpensive.

CHECKLIST

Ballpoint pen
Steel ruler
Craft knife
"C" clamps
Hammer
Scraper

Router

See pages 8-9

Veneering an edged panel

1 Select a piece of veneer slightly larger than the edged groundwork (SEE EDGE TREATMENTS). Use veneer tape to bind any splits in the veneer by taping the outer side. Place the edged panel over the veneer mounted on a backing board and mark the perimeter.

2 Using a steel straightedge and a sharp marking knife, carefully cut the veneer about ⅛ inch outside the marked line. It is important to cut across the grain first as this is most likely to split.

By using the marking knife at a shallow angle with the index finger applying firm pressure, the action is firm and slow, especially at the end of the cut where the grain is likely to break out. The blade at this point is almost horizontal.

Veneering a curved surface with contact cement

Veneering curved work, especially larger work, is normally done with curved formers or cauls using white or yellow, or plastic resin glue under pressure. For smaller work contact cement is both quick and convenient, but it does tend to shrink over a period of time.

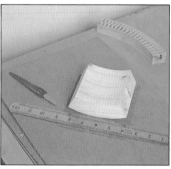

1 Select a piece of veneer to be glued to the curved work and cut it slightly oversize with the marking knife and steel ruler.

3 Now prepare a flat clamping caul: get ready some "C" clamps and place paper under the groundwork; apply white or yellow glue with a spatula. Sometimes groundwork is "keyed" (roughened up) with a toothing plane or saw edge, but it is not necessary with modern glues. The spatula here is serrated to help spread the glue evenly.

4 The white or yellow glue is left to dry for a few minutes to allow water to evaporate before the veneer is placed over the groundwork. This is to prevent glue stains from coming through the veneer, or excessive water buckling the veneer which is still possible even when it is under pressure in the clamped caul.

5 Mount the veneered panel against one or two flat cauls and clamp up so that the pressure is even. Allow to dry overnight or at least two hours under pressure at 60°F.

6 When the veneered panel is dry, the oversize veneer is carefully trimmed with the marking knife against a backing board. Tilt the panel with a spacer to transfer pressure at the knife cut.

The veneered panel is now ready for sanding (see ABRADING) or SCRAPING.

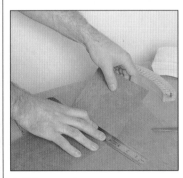

2 When cutting veneer you can cut halfway through, then break the fibers by lifting the veneer against the straightedge for a clean cut.

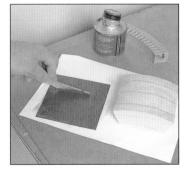

3 Use a spatula to apply the contact cement thinly on both surfaces and allow to dry for a few minutes. Always remember to replace the lid of the glue container immediately after use to prolong the life of the glue.

4 As both surfaces are brought together, the bond is instant. On larger work, a paper spacer can be used to help align the veneer with the groundwork. Press down hard against a flat surface.

5 A pressing block can be used by hand or with the aid of a hammer to ensure perfect contact between the veneer and the groundwork.

Veneering adjacent surfaces on curved groundwork

  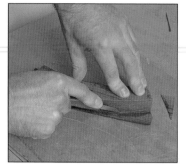 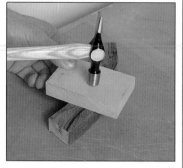

1 The convex surface of the groundwork can be carefully trimmed with the marking knife, ensuring support is given to the fibers at the point of the knife cut.

The concave surface is more tricky, and the veneer overlap may need paring back with the knife, taking care not to split the fibers.

2 Sandpaper can help to finally flatten the surfaces ready for veneering.

3 Glue the veneer with contact cement as previously described and trim afterward with the marking knife against a backing board.

4 A hammer and scrap block can help bond the veneer.

Clean up using a sanding block and make the edge slightly radiused so that the thickness of the veneer is not apparent.

Applying an edging strip to a curved surface

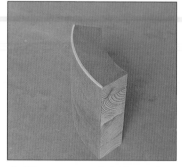

2 If the curvature is fairly gentle, the edging strip can be glued in place using masking tape as a clamping method. More severe curves can be achieved by pre-bending the edging strip, for instance by microwave heating (see BENDING WOOD).

Once the glue has set, remove the tape. Sand the edging or scrape it flush with the veneer, which is then ready for finishing.

1 This applies to straight work also, but the principle is that two adjacent veneered surfaces may need reinforcing with small solid wood edging which, in contrasting wood, can add visual interest.

Use a router (see ROUTING) with a fence and straight bit to rout a small rabbet around the curved edge to accommodate the edging strip.

Applying veneers, motifs and bandings to a flat panel

1 Interesting effects can be made by laying veneers. Here a small panel is quarter-matched and bandings added. Cut the veneer using a marking knife and backing board, and use the veneer sheet as a marker for the other pieces required.

2 Very carefully trim, join, and trim the four matching pieces using veneer tape. Also tape any splits in the veneer. Replace any severed pieces with veneer tape. Veneer tape is dampened (you can lick it) and is removed easily by further dampening after the panel has been glued.

3 Decorative motifs can be purchased in a variety of shapes, sizes, and patterns. This oval motif is laid onto the center of the quarter-veneered panel with its paper backing uppermost.

4 Carefully cut through the veneer by tracing with the marking knife on a backing board. The motif is fitted inside the opening, taped down, and glued to the panel using paper, cauls, and clamps. The groundwork is cut large to accommodate a banding strip.

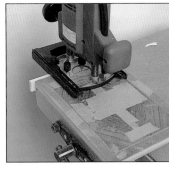

5 To border the veneered panel, a cross banding is cut with the grain running "shortwise" for decorative effect.

Cut strips of veneer for the cross banding, joining with tape where necessary to achieve the desired length. First trim the edges of the veneered panel to form a parallel border around the panel. The miters can be cut by laying the bandings in situ and carefully cutting through both together. Glue cross bandings separately, using veneer tape and flat cauls.

6 Narrow strips in varying patterns of short-grained wood sections can add enormous visual interest to a veneered panel.

After the cross bandings have been glued and dried, the veneered panel is ready for inlaying the stringing. Using the straight fence, a router can be used to rout a very fine groove around the panel (see ROUTING). Take great care with narrow cutters as they are very fragile. The depth of the groove is just under $1/12$ inch.

7 The radiused corners of the routed grooves are straightened up with a chisel (see CHISELING). Carefully cut the string by marking the mitered joints with a chisel. Then cut the stringings to the marked line against a backing board.

Use a spatula or brush to apply a little white or yellow glue into the grooves and carefully inset the stringings. A pin hammer can be used to press the stringings into place.

8 After gluing, the panel is ready for the satisfying part – the cleaning up; this is best done with a cabinet scraper (see SCRAPING). First the veneer tape is moistened with a damp cloth and then scraped away to reveal the beauty of the wood underneath. The scraper is used in all directions, but take care to work with the grain or diagonally to maintain a smooth cut. Although veneer is very thin, it is remarkable how it stands up to being scraped. The panel is now ready for FINISHING.

Wooden objects are not only esthetically pleasing, they are often useful; and the imaginative expression of technique in their making can be an important aspect of their function. Most pieces express a number of techniques, and whether a piece is intended to be a visual feast or a subtle understatement of form and material, the importance of technique cannot be over-emphasized.

There is nothing more inspirational than to look at the work of the masters of technique. The objects illustrated in this section, which include tables, cabinets, chests, chairs and decorative items, have been chosen because they express some of the techniques described in the first part of the book and because they show some of the almost limitless possibilities that exist in their creative application.

THEMES

CABINETS AND CHESTS

A cabinet or chest is usually a box with four sides, a back, and some kind of lid. Some cabinets are raised on legs to a more convenient practical height.

"Cabinetry" is a woodworking term which refers to a broad vocabulary of techniques centering around carcass work and panel and frame construction. The most common cabinet carcass is a four-sided solid wood box construction jointed together with dovetails. A cabinet can also be machine jointed and made of a veneered manufactured board such as particle board or MDF. There is a lot you can do with a box construction to turn it into an interesting cabinet. A variety of different joints, either exposed or hidden, can hold the box together at its corners. The doors can be hinged using different methods or designed to open, close, and lock in a completely novel way. The internal detailing of the cabinet can introduce an inner wealth of craftsmanship and interest revealed once the doors are opened. Some cabinets are deliberately ornate and decorative, such as those of the Art Nouveau period; others are subtle and understated, often revealing an element of surprise. Some rely on a combination of woods for their visual appeal, or they reveal a fragrant woody smell when drawers are opened.

Drawer-making is the high art of cabinet-making, and the real test of a craftsperson. Curiously there may be plenty of "different" chairs, tables, and other objects; but when it comes to cabinet drawers, traditional methods are invariably preferred. The drawer has to be made with precision, so that it glides in and out, creating a "piston" effect as it compresses the air within the carcass. Traditional drawers are time-consuming, and those masters of perfection are often masters of speed.

The cabinet employs the logic of much woodworking technique and the respective tools – flat panels jointed at right angles, parallel surfaces clamped together with ease, and square edges checked with squaring tools; for this reason cabinet-making is at the heart of woodworking, and indeed a cabinet is a pleasurable object both to possess and to make.

PAUL GOWER
Household chest
An unusual but entirely functional chest depicting a woman hitching up her skirt to reveal a little leg. The legs are patinated copper, while the carcass is Douglas fir, which has been sand-blasted to create some interesting textural contrasts. The lid HINGES to reveal an interior that follows the curves of the base.

ALAN PETERS
Chest of drawers
This chest of drawers was made of solid ash, with fumed and natural acacia wood used for the drawer fronts. The overall piece not only balances the functional requirements of the piece with a simple, understated form, but also enhances the qualities of the wood. Note how the concave rails offer a finger grip for the drawers and add visual interest. There is also real pleasure to be gained in opening the drawers and appreciating the precision with which they fit.

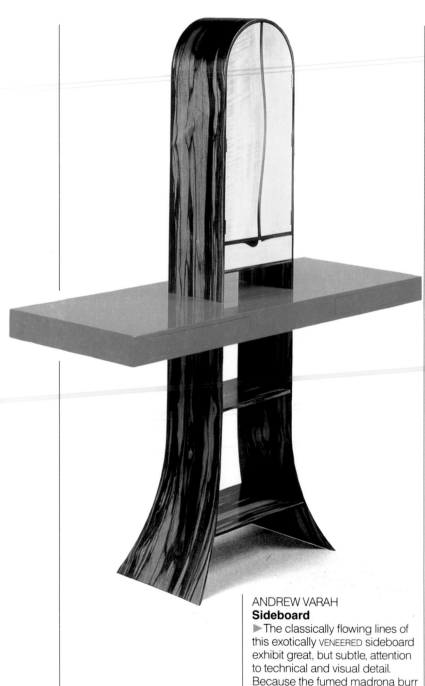

JOHN MAKEPEACE
Cabinet

◄Macassar ebony and holly were used for this striking cabinet, which combines the techniques of BENDING WOOD, solid wood construction, and high-glaze finishing. The red lacquered top is made of MDF, and the carcass is laminated. The natural grain of the wood is a surprising contrast with the bold color, while the strong geometrical shape, relieved by the wavy line at the meeting of the doors, reveals a confident use of technique and visual form.

JOHN COLEMAN
Chest of drawers

►The clean lines and simple geometric shapes of this chest of drawers reveal the architectural influences that have affected the designer's work. Every component is of equal importance, and the careful selection of materials and the planning and execution of the piece are evident in the detail of the perfectly continuing grain configuration on the drawer fronts. The piece is VENEERED in pickled oak, and it has ebony handles and japanned (lacquered) feet. The MITER JOINTS on the carcass are veneered over an MDF base, which is BISCUIT JOINTED together.

ANDREW VARAH
Sideboard

►The classically flowing lines of this exotically VENEERED sideboard exhibit great, but subtle, attention to technical and visual detail. Because the fumed madrona burr veneered door fronts are likely to pull and, therefore, bow, the same kind of wood has been used as a balancing veneer on the other side.

TERRIE NOLL
Cabinet
▲This technically ambitious piece captures perfectly the wonderfully extravagant spirit of art nouveau.

The flowing lines of the solid wood SHAPING extend to every corner of the piece, and the door includes intricate HINGES AND LOCKS. The glass shelves are appropriately subtle.

JOHN COLEMAN
Chest of drawers
◄The designer of this apparently plain piece has shown a sensitivity to the materials, technique, and form at his disposal. The silk-like character of the VENEERED figured makore carcass and drawer fronts is beautifully used, while the delicate handles and square legs enhance the geometry of the design. The success of the piece depends on the exquisite use of technique.

JOHN MAKEPEACE
Cabinet
▲This cabinet in solid wenge, vellum, and ivory is a good example of innovative cabinetmaking of its time. The designer has exposed the sides of the drawers within a "skeleton" framework of posts and drawer runners. Unlike traditional drawers, which rely on lapped DOVETAILS at the front and through-dovetails at the rear, these employ through-dovetails and a shaped detail to emphasize the joint.

ROBERT INGHAM
Chest of drawers
The visual and tactile qualities of solid ripple sycamore have been exploited by great technical skill in the execution of this simple concept. The titanium handles, which form a delicate contrast to the solid appearance of the wood, provide additional visual interest, while the unusually SHAPED corners of the drawers and the complementary framework contribute subtly to the overall success of the piece.

PAUL ROCHON
Cabinet

This intricately engineered bow-fronted cocktail cabinet is a virtual treasury of woods, incorporating lacewood (plane), Australian walnut, African cherry, cocobolo rosewood, ebony, holly, maple, padauk, and purpleheart. The lacewood doors conceal a pull-out container for bottles, and internal mechanisms, made of wood, lift and slide to operate the various storage compartments.

JEREMY BROUN
Cabinet

▶ This pyramidal corner cabinet uses several power-tool techniques, including SAWING, PLANING, and ROUTING to combine VENEERED and solid wood. From a single 2-inch board of ash, ⅛-inch veneers were cut with a bandsaw and planer-thicknesser, and the matching veneers were laid on the plywood panels that form the carcass. The doors were cut away with a jigsaw and their edges mitered with hidden bandings (EDGE TREATMENTS) using a router. The piece is unusual in having no handles. Access to the 13 bottles and glasses that it contains is by means of the pivoting center flap.

WALES & WALES
Cabinet

▶ This striking nine-drawer cabinet is based on a deceptively simple idea. It is made of fumed and natural oak. The solid wood carcass is mitered, BISCUIT JOINTED, and tenoned together, and the side-hung drawers are DOVETAILED. The front is constructed from solid slats, which were glued to the solid drawer fronts. The cupboard doors are VENEERED, and the back of the carcass is veneered in bog oak. The small drawers, which are opened by means of spring-loaded catches, are finished with melamine lacquer and decorated with gold leaf and paint. It is an excellent example of the technique of EDGE-JOINTING.

PHILIP KOOMEN
Cabinet

▶ This cabinet is designed to house a television, video recorder, and cassettes in three separate compartments, which are divided by HINGED flaps. It is VENEERED in English walnut on a laminboard base and has solid walnut bandings (EDGE TREATMENTS). The door panels, which are of yew and have walnut moldings, form a grid pattern and use MITER JOINTS.

KAREN M. HANSEN
Shelving unit
Ash and beech were used to create this unusual unit, which was devised to be both sturdy and easy to dismantle. The design was created to take advantage of the qualities of green and air-dried timber that had been harvested from coppice and first thinnings. The framework is made from ash logs, finished by burning and polishing, and the whole piece is assembled with wedge joints at each corner. The wedging brackets can be plain, or they can be decorated to express a theme.

LUCINDA LEECH
Display case
A display cabinet in ash and wenge. Specially designed to display a gallery's collection of ceramics or glass, this crisp, elegant display unit is as versatile as it is utilitarian. The top section can be separated from the bottom section to create two separate display units. The design is airy and understated, allowing the pieces to be displayed at maximum exposure. (Commissioned by the Artizana Gallery.)

CHAIRS AND BENCHES

Aristotle was happy to sit on a boulder while thinking his thoughts, and ever since then, mankind has sat upon everything conceivable.

The chair is probably the most over-designed object in history, and to this day it is still regarded as the ultimate challenge for designers. The great architects of the world have tried their skills at designing chairs – Le Corbusier, Alvar Aalto, Charles Eames. It has been said that a designer's reputation can be made for a decade if he or she creates a new chair, but if it is comfortable, then it is a bonus.

The wooden chair is particularly challenging as not only is the material appropriately tactile for such an object, but the strength requirements can easily result in an over-engineered and visually confusing design, so the designer has to know the material well.

To produce a wooden chair which satisfies the criteria of adequate body support, soundness of construction, simple, elegant understated lines, and a clear expression of technique and material is a tall order, and very few chairs pass the test. A well-known designer once said, "There has to be a very good reason for me to design a chair." That reason is often to do with technique or technical revolution – a new way of using the material.

In this selection of chairs, classic designs have been included which are particularly significant from a technique point of view: Michael Thonet's "café society" chair of the mid-19th century exploited wood bending; Alvar Aalto's laminated designs of the 1930s were inspired by trees bending in the wind; Hans Wegner's chair of 1949 employed a variety of techniques and successfully married handicraft traditions with industrial production.

Today's "designer" chairs tend to be more self-expressive, and there is no major design style or technical innovation emerging which can be seen as coming anywhere near the importance of the examples mentioned above. But the challenge to produce new and interesting chairs is as great as ever, and this selection shows a few examples of chairs which explore technique as a major part of their *raison d'être*.

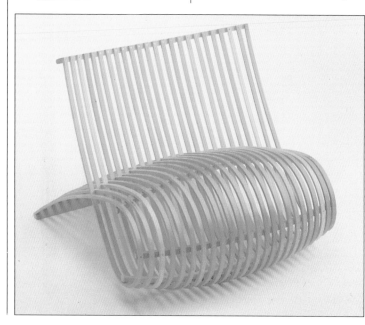

MARC NEWSON
Chair
◄ Simple in design and concept, this sculptural chair in beech heartwood offers the viewer visual pleasure from any angle. The flowing lines belie the considerable technical achievement required in BENDING WOOD to such extremes.

ALVAR AALTO
Chair
► This classically formed chair is a perfect example of BENDING WOOD. It was created in 1936-7 by Alvar Aalto, the famous Modernist designer, and produced by the Finnish company Artek, which was founded by Aalto and his wife. The bending of the sections of birch stretches wood laminating technology to the limit in the formation of the long, cantilevered shape, and the technique wholly dictates the form. Any decoration to enhance the timeless qualities of the design would be entirely superfluous.

POUL KJAERHOLM
Theater seating
▶ The waves of the sea are reflected in the design of this seating for a theater in Louisiana, northern Denmark. The designer has not only suited the chair to the environment but also to the user, because the woven ash seat and back construction overcomes the problem of creaking.

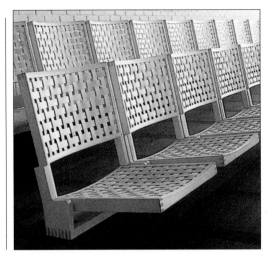

JEREMY BROUN
Stool

▼ The inspiration behind this small stool or table is the Scandinavian tradition of BENDING WOOD. It was made from a continuous piece of ash, steam bent by means of a kitchen kettle, and using ROUTING techniques and simple JIGMAKING. The wood at the bend itself was reduced so that it could be shaped over a simple jig, but the bend was restrengthened by the solid mahogany inserts, which were routed in diagonally using another jig. The resulting structure was routed away at the edges to expose the finger inserts and to enhance the form.

HANS J. WEGNER
Chair

▶ The commanding lines of this superbly made ash and teak chair embrace several interesting techniques. BENDING WOOD was used to achieve the laminated curve, while the SHAPED "peacock feathers" enter the seat with DOWEL JOINTS. The legs and cross-rails use TURNING. Although this chair was made in Denmark, it is in many ways similar to the classic English Windsor chair.

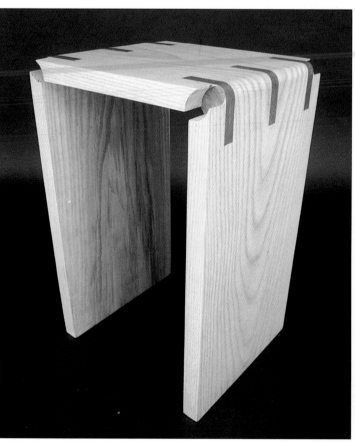

HANS J. WEGNER
Valet chair

This chair is typical of Danish mass-produced furniture that is based on the tradition of hand-crafted pieces. It was originally designed in 1953, but the design is timeless. It is made by a careful combination of hand and machine techniques, especially the time-consuming finishing stages. The grain is raised by wetting, and fine ABRADING is used.

ROBERT WILLIAMS
Chair
◀These distinctive plank-backed chairs were designed in 1977 and are excellent examples of a variety of techniques. The chairs, which were made in solid oak, ash, or sycamore, employ BENDING techniques in the laminated back and ROUTING for dishing the seat. Finger JOINTS are used at the front of the seat, and MORTISE-AND-TENON JOINTS at the rear. GLUING and assembly are done by hand, as is the finishing. The chairs rely on JIGMAKING throughout, and despite the batch-production methods employed in their manufacture, these chairs still exhibit tremendous individuality, not least in the careful selection of materials.

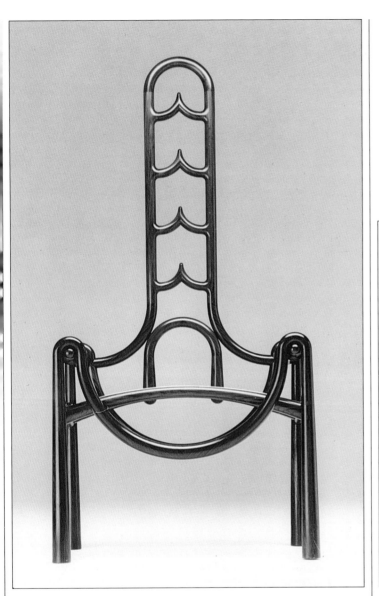

ANDREW VARAH
Chair
▲Meticulous craftsmanship has been combined with a flowing form to create this unusual chair, which is made of Indian rosewood and has a woven cane seat. The chair is made mainly from BENDING techniques applied to solid wood, and the designer has cleverly overcome the problem of "short grain." Note how the circular sectioned members diminish in size, adding further complexity to the making. Although it is not clear from the photograph, the deeply bowed front under-rail slants inward so that it clears the sitter's legs.

JEREMY BROUN
Chair
Solid wood JOINTING techniques achieved this simple organic form, inspired by the lines of classic Scandinavian furniture. The wood, American ash, was stained indigo. The woven sailing cord upholstery relies on simple DRILLING with a small bench-mounted drill.

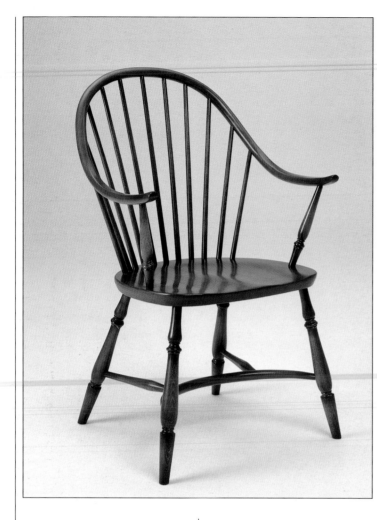

ERCOL FURNITURE LTD.
Chair
The Windsor chair is perhaps the best known English chair, and its origins, although uncertain, probably lie in the mid-18th century. Countless variations of the style are still being made. "Windsor" is a generic term, used to describe chairs of stick construction, but the distinctive style employs BENDING by steaming ash and yew. The technique of TURNING WOOD is used for the legs and back members, which are DOWEL JOINTED into the SHAPED seat.

HANS J. WEGNER
Chair
Made of oak and with a seat of woven cane, the flowing back and arms of this classic chair are an object lesson in wood SHAPING, while the overall construction relies on intricate JOINTS. Originally designed in 1947, this chair is another example of Danish mass-produced articles based on the tradition of hand-crafted work. Note how the curved front-rail enters the wider round sectioned leg with a recessed shouldered MORTISE-AND-TENON JOINT.

POUL KJAERHOLM
Chair
▶This innovative chair is formed from the technique of BENDING using an improved steam-bending method whereby the cells in the wood are compressed and made highly pliable so that they can be formed into virtually any shape, including tied knots. The wood remains pliable for as long as it is moist.

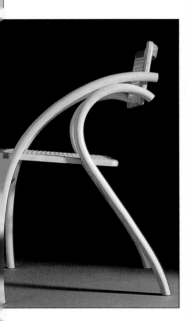

BEN HEAF
Chair
▲The laminated construction of this elegant and sophisticated chair uses BENDING techniques. It is made of ash throughout and has a woven cane seat. The section of the laminated members is circular.

MICHAEL THONET
Chair
◀ This classic chair was designed by the German craftsman Michael Thonet, who was working in Austria in the mid-19th century, and it marked a milestone in the development of woodworking techniques. Its radical shape relies entirely on steam BENDING.
The plywood seat, which may be up to 2 inches thick, is formed in one continuous bend, which pushed the bending technique to the limit. Its superb visual lines, comfort, and economic use of wood have made it probably one of the most copied chairs ever to have been produced.

SAMUEL CHAN
Chair
▶ The pleasing and subtle mixture of Oriental and Occidental influences evident in this chair combines with a practicality of construction that allows for ease of manufacture and for strength. The chair shown here is made from beech veneer, although a Formica version has been made.

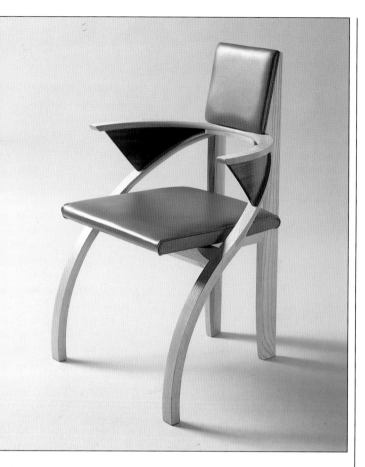

CHRISTOPHER ROSE
Dining chair
▲ The leather upholstery in either matching or contrasting colors gives this ash-framed chair an individuality to suit the mood of the owner. The frame is available in either natural or black lacquer to further expand the choice, and the matched or contrasted wood panels below the arms offer yet more possible variations.

STEFAN DURING
Bench settee
◀Not all modern chairs are uncomfortable. The flowing elegance of this two-seater settee focuses attention on the constructional techniques of the meeting of the curved back members with the arm rests, which enables the user to slouch into the corner, or into the back or the side, at will. The settee is made of ash and employs BENDING techniques in the steam-bent curved members, which are jointed with MORTISE-AND-TENON JOINTS. It is upholstered in leather.

TERRIE NOLL
Bench
The designer of this magnificent art nouveau-style bench used modern electric carving tools to shape the intricately woven patterns in the mahogany. The finishing was, however, by hand ABRADING. The end panels are VENEERED in blistered mahogany.

TABLES AND DESKS

A table is a flat supporting surface at a given height depending on its function. The dining table has been described as the social center of the home. It is where much learning occurs, views are exchanged, and where family social interaction takes place as a daily ritual. The conference table is usually larger and more prestigious in construction and form, and allows interaction in a more deliberately structured way – the circular conference table is "democratic" as it allows all members to feel they are equal. The coffee table may be the only hand-crafted item in an interior full of mass-produced objects. It might be highly individual or quite plain and subdued.

The table offers a challenge to the woodworker. In order to achieve a supporting surface at a given height, there are numerous construction options beyond simply placing one leg at each corner. Consider the problem in terms of a space to be filled by a structure, which draws on a wide vocabulary of woodworking techniques. This is what makes designing so exciting – putting aside preconceptions about the way a piece should look or whether it should rely on traditional constructions. Instead you identify a series of problems, set down criteria which must be met, and then consider the most appropriate techniques to use.

Some tables in this selection explore particular conceptual or technical themes of interest to those designers or perhaps the clients for whom the tables were intended. Some examples are relatively easy to make and others deceptively simple-looking. A table is an excellent object for a relative beginner because its main elements need only be a supporting structure for a flat top. The top could be made of MDF with its edges banded, and the legs could be of a standard section employing simple joints. However simple in form or construction your table is, it needs to be made well, and the foundation of its success is the command of technique.

SAMUEL CHAN
Table

▶This table-cum-storage unit pays homage to the work of the Modernist designer Gerrit Rietveld, although its straight line and simple form are timeless. The woodworking techniques include traditional Japanese joints in the mahogany frame, while DOVETAIL JOINTS are used in the sycamore hanging boxes.

NICHOLAS MEECH
Table
▶This original table is based on a traditional technique – that of forming circular dowel through a dowelplate from a rough timber section (DOWEL JOINTS). The natural stick has been fashioned in a slightly contrived way with a rotary handplane (PLANING).

JOHN MAKEPEACE
Petra serving table
◀The aura of a piece of furniture can be created by the light falling upon it. Light is an important element in three-dimensional design, creating shadow and enhancing form, line, and texture. Here the designer has used the simple theme of a stack of regular boxes to create irregularity. The boundaries of utilitarian furniture and fine art have been crossed making this piece different from much hand-made furniture today.

FRED BAIER
Desk

▶ The idea underlying the design of this desk was to construct a piece that could be simply made by someone with little formal woodworking training. The piece shown here is made of stained sycamore, with VENEERED surface work in plywood. The sycamore has been stained with a xylene dye and a pre-catalyzed lacquer sprayed on. BISCUIT JOINTS are employed throughout.

STEPHEN FIELD
Table

◀ This elegant Pembroke table is made of satinwood with a broad inlaid band of purpleheart and additional cross-banding in Rio rosewood. The square-section tapering legs, which are inlaid with lines of ebony, have collars at the ankles and are mounted on brass castors. The drawer is lined with cedarwood. The top was made up of five strips of solid Brazilian mahogany, with the heart side placed alternately up and down. After gluing and leveling, this was counter-VENEERED with Honduras mahogany, placed so that the grain direction lies at right angles to that of the solid wood. The satinwood was laid with a balancing veneer underneath. The flaps were made in the same way, which, although time-consuming, does mean that the piece is completely stable. The rule JOINTS were cut before the lengthy process of cutting and inlaying the purpleheart and rosewood began. The carcass and legs were made of solid Brazilian mahogany.

PAUL GOWER
Work station
Made of scrubbed and bleached English oak, this kitchen work station has a gently curved top. The design was inspired partly by the undulating form of Chinese roofs and partly by the shape of a butcher's block, which helps to impart a "kitchen" feel to the piece. The chopping boards and central knife drawer are of end grain maple, while the trays at each side are of stainless steel.

NEIL CLARKE

Desk

This lustrous desk is made from solid North American cherry and maple. Several woodworking techniques were employed in its construction. A variety of DOVETAIL JOINTS has been used in the carcass, and MORTISE-AND-TENON JOINTS were utilized in the construction of the underframe and of the stool. A finish of Danish oil was used to enhance the qualities of the natural wood.

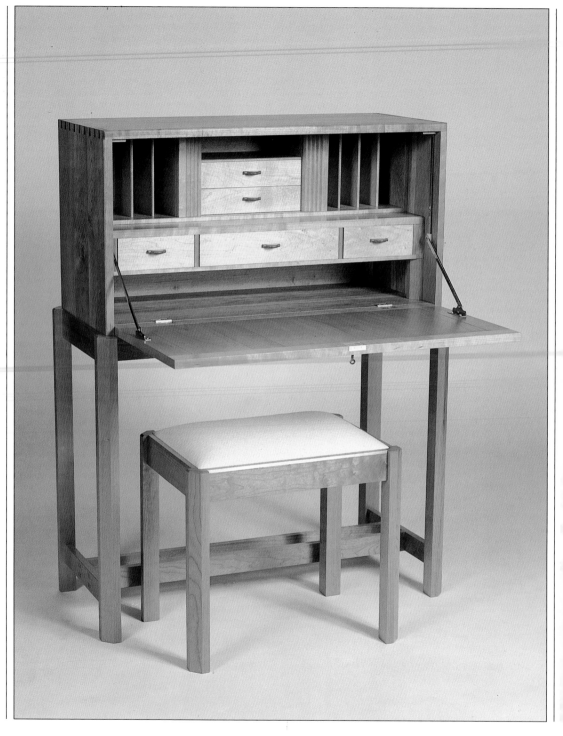

DEREK S. DAVIS
Desk
▼A simple concept has produced a space-age writing desk. The wood used was American hard maple, and the writing panel was VENEERED with blistered maple. The detailing is walnut. The legs were DOWEL JOINTED, blocked, and screwed. The drawers have DOVETAIL JOINTS, and the veneer was pressed using platens. The desk was finished with several coats of oil and polyurethane, with beeswax melted into the blend for the last three coats.

ALAN PETERS
Table
▼This low table is made of solid Andaman padauk with contrasting sycamore uprights, and it uses that most distinguishable of woodworking joints, the DOVETAIL. Here, however, the joint in the top is echoed in the section of the vertical members. Because the direction of the grain is similar in all the components, the table will move freely as the ambient humidity changes. A subtle shoulder has been incorporated into the vertical rails to give strength to the top.

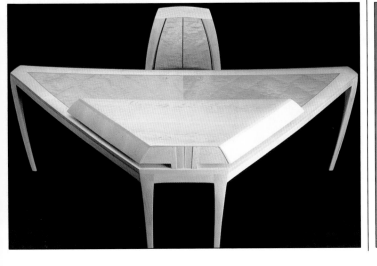

DEREK PEARCE
Table
▶The top of this unusual library table is made of two pieces of Colombian pine, BISCUIT JOINTED together. The end piece was cut off and joined to the top with a hand-cut through-DOVETAIL JOINT. The "books" are made from various woods, including plywood, MDF, pine, and hardwood, which were attached at the top with two lengths of ½-inch studding and theater "boss" plates. The realistic appearance of the books was achieved with a variety of techniques and tools, including the use of the router, shoulder plane, circular saw, and chainsaw. They were finished with stains, inks, and a blowtorch to give the desired book-like effect, while the table top was sprayed with satin finish and a heat- and scratch-resistant polyurethane.

BEN BROOKS
Table

This low table was conceived to express the turbulence of flowing water, and the designer made numerous abstract drawings from life to capture the dynamic movements he wanted to represent in the piece. The selection of materials was also a crucial part of the design process. The top and back legs are of English oak, inlaid with sycamore. The under-structure is made of thin laminated sheets of oak, distorted and held in torsion without having to be steam bent or laminated over a former.

WALES & WALES
Table

▶This elegant design resolves the recurrent problem of how to support a circular table top with three legs by translating the traditional theme of a tripod construction into a modern vernacular. The underframe, which is a good example of BENDING WOOD, is laminated in ash and is connected by dowels into turned wood blocks. The ash VENEERED top is prominently banded with cherry (EDGE TREATMENTS).

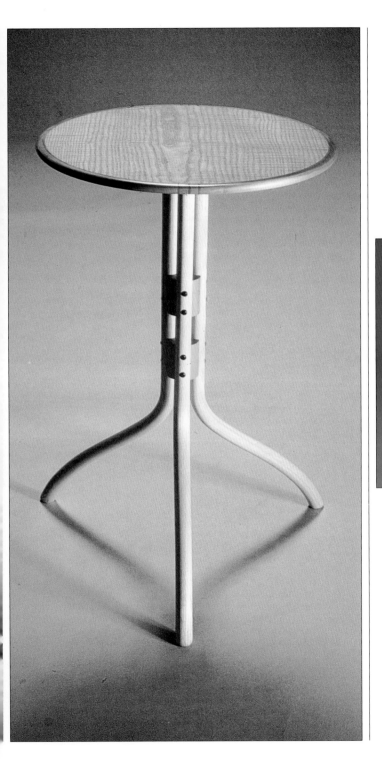

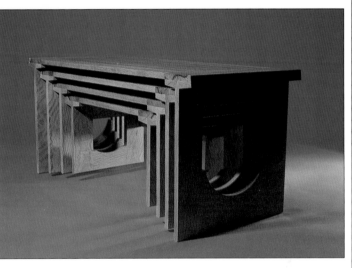

EDWARD HOPKINS
Nesting tables
The simple but excellently
executed design allows the quality
of the materials to shine through.
The bold frame and panel
construction includes the use of
large MORTISE-AND-TENON JOINTS,
and the medullary ray of evergreen
oak is especially eye-catching here.
The superb construction allows
each table to be slid smoothly out
along its HOUSING with just one hand.

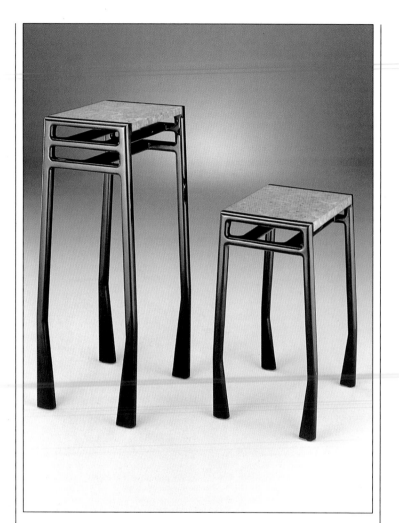

PETER CZUK
Tables
This pair of maple burl tables have been created in much the same way that a jeweler might set a precious stone. The base and top of each piece are carefully balanced to form one complete whole. The tops are single pieces of solid maple burl, approximately 1 inch thick, and they are removable, being held in place by spring-loaded bullet latches, which allow the burl to expand and contract independently of the base. The designer employed MORTISE-AND-TENON JOINTS in the legs, and black lacquer finishing.

LUKE HUGHES
Desk
A special commission from a client who wanted to be able to spread out his copy of the *Financial Times* without impediment. This pleasingly proportioned desk in English oak with rosewood details has DOVETAILED cedar-bottomed drawers which smell sweetly when opened. The whole creation can be flatpacked for ease of transportation.

ALAN PETERS
Table
This elegant fluted fan table, which is made of solid Indian rosewood inlaid with sycamore,
is a clever example of fine SHAPING and PLANING. Each flute is a separate tapered piece of wood, constructed in a JIG. After the fluting and inlaying processes, the sections were jointed and GLUED together.

MICHAEL FORTUNE
Table

▶ This highly sculptural living room table is made from an exotic combination of woods: blistered maple, ebony, dyed maple, and purpleheart. Introducing shapes or curves (SHAPING WOOD) into furniture offers opportunities for visual interest, but often at the expense of placing considerable technical demands on the maker. This technically complex piece demonstrates the use of ROUTING, BISCUIT JOINTING, and solid and VENEERED construction.

JEREMY BROUN
Table

◀ This unusual table is made of solid bubinga, and its construction employs several techniques, including the unusual "zigzag" JOINT at the center. The concept of the three arms of laminated solid strips (PLANING) that meet in the center dictates the shape of the jointed intersection, which is cut by careful hand SAWING and power tool (ROUTING) methods. A stout "loose" tongue (EDGE-JOINTING) binds the center joint together. Massive milled joints are used at the corners, and all joints are highlighted with a 1/16-inch routed groove.

WOODWORK
DECORATIVE

The term decorative is used rather loosely here to describe a category of wooden objects which happen to fall outside the other, more clearly defined categories chosen for this book.

To decorate is to adorn or embellish with ornament. It is a term which tends to refer to the somewhat superfluous method of styling, notably of past work which at best includes highly skilled carving or fretwork, and at worst can be a visual disguise for inadequate structure or inappropriate constructional technique. However, the term decorative has a more modern and broader connotation, referring to objects which are primarily designed to please the eye or generally stimulate the senses, perhaps objects whose main function is to adorn the functional environment.

Chairs, tables, and cabinets are more clearly understood as functional or utilitarian objects, although some examples are highly decorative or possess a sculptural quality. When talking of function, it is limiting to consider just one function or purpose. A chair may be primarily for sitting on, but visual appeal is extremely important, too.

The contemporary woodworker may be working to please him or herself or specifically to a client's brief, and in our consumer society, where increased automation may give vast choice at a relatively low price, the decorative craft object addresses the problem of depersonalization. In some extreme cases, this may have led to over-indulgent craftsmanship, but at best it expresses the pure beauty of wood and an appropriate level of technique for the particular object.

The items chosen in this section are varied in nature and express the richness of wood and its fashioning techniques. The trend toward decorative woodwork where the function of a piece extends traditional boundaries is an interesting one, and inevitably, because of the human input and rarity of wood used, many decorative objects are expensive and beyond the reach or touch of ordinary people. It is indeed a very lucky person who can thus acquire the skill to produce such objects, irrespective of whether they sell or not.

TOM RAUSCHKE/KAAREN WIKEN
Bowl
This unusual bowl features a reversible top, one side of which represents a winter landscape, the other a summer landscape. The outer bowl shape was turned on a lathe from a solid hickory log, and then cut with a jeweler's saw before being hand-carved to make what might have been a simple, functional container into a unique piece. The removable landscape cover was created using marquetry techniques. The summer fields are made from black walnut, lignum vitae, maple, Osage orange, ash, and ebony; while the snow-capped details on the winter scene are made from holly. The lignum vitae trees were turned on a lathe before being milled on a drill press. Kaaren Wiken's embroidery of the reflected sky is contained under the glass-topped "pond."

TOBY WINTERINGHAM
Trays

These attractive and colorful VENEERED trays emphasize the tactile quality of wood. They incorporate decorative motifs, which are inlaid at the center into veneers glued onto MDF (medium density fiberboard). The outer rims are made of English cherry, and they are finished with catalyzed lacquer.

JEFF KEMP
Guitar

▶ The construction of a classical guitar embodies the greatest possible variety of woodworking techniques. From the EDGE-JOINTING of the wafer-thin cedarwood face, the SHAPING of the underface struts, and the BENDING by heat of the cocobolo rosewood sides, to the ABRADING of the sculpted neck and DRILLING of the head for the machine heads. Any luthier knows, however, that the moment of truth depends not on whether the joints are tight and the glue lines almost invisible or whether the neck is perfectly in line with the face – although these are important, of course – but on whether the instrument has the right sound when it is first plucked. Even then, the quality of the sound may depend on the finishing.

JEREMY TURNER
Dish

◄This attractive low-relief dish was carved from sycamore. The leaf design was drawn on using a cardboard template. After the carving was completed, the dish was washed to clean it and to raise the grain. When it was dry, the roughened surface was rubbed smooth before being painted with watercolors. Several layers of paint were applied to achieve the desired density of color. It was then rubbed lightly to remove a little of the color in order to highlight the edges and the texture of the carved surface. Finally, two coats of catalyzed lacquer were applied, each layer being rubbed back with steel wool when set, and the finished piece was polished with beeswax.

TOBIAS KAYE
Sounding bowl

This sounding bowl in cherry is one in a series which Kaye creates by TURNING. When forming these delightful pieces, Kaye pays great attention to the "acoustic curve," listening as well as using his eyes and hands to assess its harmony of form. If these acoustic bowls are to be successful, the thickness of the walls have to be one-eightieth or one-fiftieth of the diameter, depending on whether the bowl is deep or shallow. Strings are fed through brass tubing inserted in the bowl walls; this brightens the tone and prevents them from cutting along the grain.

BERT MARSH
Vase

This beautifully grained vase was made from a small part of a complete laburnum log. The white round top and base are made of the sapwood, which goes around the log, leaving the heartwood in the center. The vase, which was TURNED on a lathe, is shaped to exploit the natural annual rings of the wood.

DEEP SPRING STUDIO
Basket

▶ What is not immediately evident from the illustration is that this basket is collapsible. Different woods – padauk, ebony, and tiger maple – were laid in sequence and laminated and edge-glued to form a solid block about 1 inch deep. The handle is cut first, and then the body is cut in a continuously decreasing spiral. When the piece is folded flat, therefore, the pattern of the grain and lamination appears as a complete design over the entire surface. All the cutting is carried out with a bandsaw used free-hand. The basket is opened up by, first, gently raising the sides and then by carefully rotating the handle into position.

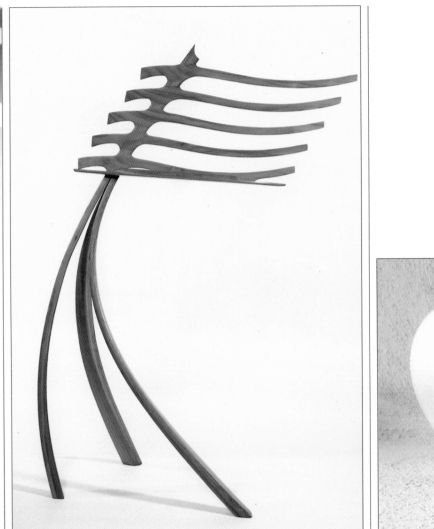

NIC PRYKE
Box
◄This unusual box is designed to hold two decanters. It is made mainly of American cherry, banded with ebony (EDGE TREATMENTS) and inlaid with sterling silver, and a variety of woods, including walnut, sycamore and burl ash. Although it is based on the traditional idea of inlaid work, it is given a modern look by the abstract motifs and patterns.

CHRISTOPHER HAUTH
Music stand
▲ Like an aspen bending in the wind, this elegant music stand in black walnut captures the force and dignity of nature in a positive and uncontrived way. Built with traditional joinery using tapered laminations, it is finished in hand-rubbed tung oil to achieve a finish in keeping with its natural theme.

TOBIAS KAYE
Bowl
▲This thin-walled bowl is made from holly wood. The form was TURNED wet – that is, while the wood was still fresh and supple – on the lathe. Holly wood becomes very white when it is dried quickly, and the bowl has been further lightened by rubbing lemon juice (citric acid) into the grain. It was intended as a purely decorative piece, and the designer's aim was to emphasize, through the strongly upward movement of the form, the delicacy of the wood. The whiteness, smooth grain, and crisp, clean cut that the wood takes from the lathe all contribute to the impression of lightness.

CHRISTOPHER HAUTH
Hall stand
◄Subtly blending the needs of form and function, this delicate hall stand is visually arresting. The low-key tung oil finish is in keeping with the fine luster of the black walnut, and the traditional joinery employed reflects the simple nature of its application.

MAX COOPER
Box
▲This gracefully rounded collector's box of VENEERED satinwood is decorated with drapes of neoclassical marquetry motifs on the curved top and sides. The doors open to reveal the six bow-fronted drawers, which are made from laminated ebony and veneered in Rio rosewood. The DOVETAIL JOINTED drawers are lined with boxwood.

BODDINGTON & FOOTE
Lectern
The lectern, which was designed to bear weights of up to 22 pounds, is made of solid African wenge. It is laminated from sawn-cut VENEERS and glued together with epoxy resin in a male and female laminating mold. The laminates are joined together with dado joints and by a stainless steel core, which is threaded through and has T-nuts on the ends. The fittings are hidden in the counter bores and covered by TURNED wenge pellets. The floor laminates have a lead core, which lowers the center of gravity. The piece was finished with a basecoat of acid-catalyzed lacquer before being burnished and waxed with teak wax.

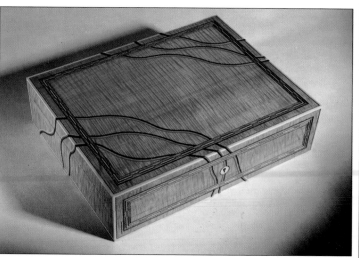

MAX COOPER
Clock

◀The marquetry case of this longcase clock is VENEERED in carefully selected English walnut on a ground of solid English oak. The marquetry, which uses 12 different woods, depicts acanthus scrolls and flowers, reminiscent of the styles of the late 17th century.

ANDREW CRAWFORD
Box

▲This striking casket, which was designed as an artist's watercolor box, is both an exhibition piece and wholly practical. The basic carcass is of birch plywood and maple, and the corner JOINTS are double rabbets. The exterior is beautifully VENEERED in Canadian maple and decorated with dyed veneers. Notice especially how the lines flow around the surface, over the boxwood edgings, and under the colorful geometric lines, changing color themselves as they do so. This idea is echoed inside the lid. The wavy lines were made by cutting thin strips from a "sandwich" of veneers, formed by laminating them in a curved former. The fitted interior includes two specially made water pots; and a small drawer with DOVETAIL JOINTS, which is opened by pulling a small, TURNED boxwood knob, contains another palette.

ROBERT INGHAM
Casket
As many as 80 small panels of burr elm held in frames of bog oak were used in the construction of this casket. The lining and trays are of ripple sycamore. The HINGES are also made of wood, while the brasswork fittings were designed and made as integral elements of the overall design.

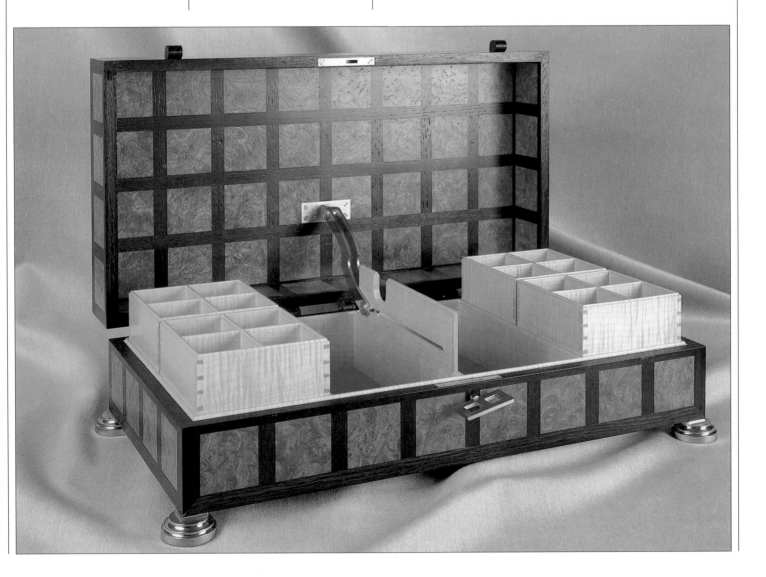

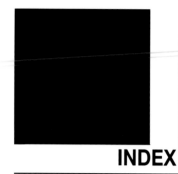

INDEX

Page numbers in italic refer to captions and illustrations.

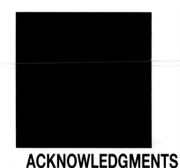

ACKNOWLEDGMENTS

Quarto would like to thank the following for all their help with this project.

(T = top; L = left; C = center; R = right; B = below; M = middle)

Page 65 John Anderson; **page 128 T** Paul Gower/Parnham College, Dorset; **page 129** Alan Peters; **page 130 L** John Makepeace Workshops, Parnham House, Dorset; **page 131 C** Andrew Varah; **page 131 TL** John Coleman; **page 131 R** Terrie Noll; **page 132 L** John Coleman; **page 132 R** John Makepeace Workshops, Parnham House, Dorset; **page 133** Robert Ingham – Principal, Parnham College, Dorset; **page 134** Paul Rochon; **page 135 L** Wales & Wales; **page 135 M** Philip Koomen Furniture; **page 135 R** Jeremy Broun; **page 136** Karen Hansen; **page 137** special commission for Artizana by Lucinda Leech; **page 138** Poul Kjaerholm; **page 139 B** Alvar Aalto/Artek; **page 139 T** Cappellini International Interiors; **page 140 L** Wegner/PP Mobler APS, Denmark; **page 140 R** Jeremy Broun; **page 141** Wegner/PP Mobler APS, Denmark; **page 142 L** Robert Williams of Pearl Dot, London; **page 143 L** Andrew Varah; **page 143 R** Jeremy Broun; **page 144 L** Ercol Furniture Limited, High Wycombe; **page 144 R** Wegner/PP Mobler APS, Denmark; **page 145 L** Ben Heaf; **page 145 R** Poul Kjaerholm/PP Mobler APS, Denmark; **page 146** Hescot Ltd, Newmarket; **page 147 L** Samuel Chan; **page 147 R** Christopher Rose of Pearl Dot, London; **page 148** Stefan During, Texel, Holland; **page 149** Terrie Noll; **page 150 T** Samuel Chan; **page 150 B** John Makepeace Workshops, Parnham House, Dorset; **page 151** Nicholas Meech; **page 152 L** Stephen Field, Cabinet Maker; **page 152 R** Fred Baier; **page 153** Paul Gower/Parnham College, Dorset; **page 154** Neil Clarke; **page 155 TL** Derek S Davis; **page 155 TR** Alan Peters; **page 155 B** commissioned by Artizana and made by Derek Pearce; **page 156** Ben Brooks/Parnham College, Dorset; **page 157 L** Wales & Wales; **page 157 R** Edward Hopkins; **page 158** Peter Czuk/The Rosen Group; **page 159** Luke Hughes & Co Ltd; **page 160** Alan Peters; **page 161 T** Michael C Fortune; **page 161 B** Jeremy Broun; **page 162 T** Tom Rauschke and Kaaren Wiken, Photography: William Lemke; **page 163 T** Toby Winteringham; **page 163 B** Jeff Kemp; **page 164 T** Jeremy Turner; **page 164 B** Tobias Kaye; **page 165 L** Bert Marsh; **page 165 B** Deep Spring Studio/The Rosen Group; **page 166** Nic Pryke, Photography: Graham Pearson; **page 167 L** Christopher Hauth; **page 167 R** Tobias Kaye; **page 168 L** Christopher Hauth; **page 168 R** Max Cooper; **page 169** special commission for Artizana by Silver Lining Workshops; **page 170 L** Max Cooper; **page 170 R** Andrew Crawford; **page 171** Robert Ingham – Principal, Parnham College, London.

We would like to thank the following contributors whose work we have featured on the jacket:
Bert Marsh; Cappellini International Interiors; Nicholas Meech; Tom Rauschke and Kaaren Wiken, Photography: William Lemke; Wegner/PPi/obler APS, Denmark.
Quarto would like to extend a special thanks to the manufacturers who kindly lent tools and materials for photography and demonstrations.
Tools supplied by:
Axminster Power Tool Centre, AEG (UK) Ltd, Black & Decker, Bosch Power Tools, Franchi Lock & Tools, Hitachi (UK) Ltd, Kity, Luna Tools Ltd (Ryobi), Makita Power Tools, Panasonic Power Tools, Record Power Tools, Skil, Stanley Tools, Trend Cutting Tools, Wolfcraft.

Materials supplied by:
The Art Veneers Company Ltd, John Boddy Timber Ltd, Oscar Windebank Ltd, Silverman's and Sons Sheet Materials, Sp Systems – Isle of Wight.